# Unshakeable You

# Unshakeable You

*Becoming your own lighthouse of certainty in an uncertain world*

NIDHI KONA

*A deep heartfelt thank you to everyone who has helped me put this creation together by offering their stories, insights, and efforts. I am eternally grateful to my dear parents, friends, and THE ONE in all of us.*

# CONTENTS

# PROLOGUE

It was a sunny morning in the summer of 2002. A seven-year-old girl lay half awake, contemplating if she should get out of bed or let sleep take her to exciting places again in her imagination. Still dazed, she hid under her blanket and chose sleep, when a sharp yet pleasant ring of a bell greeted her. "It's here!" She said as she sprang out of her bed and chased the sweet ringing of the bell. And there it was, in all its glory, her first bicycle. As the sun's rays fell upon the sturdy white handles of the bicycle and its colorful seat, it seemed as if the bicycle had an aura of its own.

"Come, let's go." her dad beckoned her with a wide smile on his face. Without wasting a second, she chased him and the bicycle onto the street. As she hopped onto the bicycle's seat, an unsettling thought hit her. "Will I fall?" she asked, still excited but also a little puzzled. Dad assured her saying "No, you won't. See you have these training wheels on the bicycle for balance."

Convinced by the explanation, she peddled away with fervor. That whole day was spent riding the bicycle whenever she got the chance. It was a lot of fun. Until it wasn't. She had gotten bored because no matter how hard she tried to peddle, the bicycle wouldn't go faster, as the training wheels kept holding her back.

When her dad returned in the evening, she told him her dilemma. "Ok then, do it without the training wheels." he said as if it was no big deal. "But I will fall! I want to go fast, but I will fall. And I don't want to fall." protested the little one. In that moment he said something that would stick with her for the rest of her life. "It doesn't matter how many times you fall. What matters is how many times you get back up." he said knowingly, dismantling the training wheels. "Ok, but it will hurt!" said the little girl. "I will hold you, don't worry. See I am holding onto your bicycle like this, you won't fall." he said gripping the tail end of her bicycle. So she rode hesitantly and stopped to say "Hold properly, Papa!"

"Yes, yes, I am, don't worry. You just have to go." he replied. With that leap of faith in his words, off she went peddling, focusing solely on the road ahead. "I can do this, I will do this, he's there for me anyway." She told herself as she tried to find her balance. The bicycle gained momentum as she gained confidence. Feeling incredibly happy, with a racing heart she exclaimed "Yay, I am doing it. I am cycling so fast like I am flying." As she turned back to smile at her dad, she saw him standing at a distance smiling. "Good job." he said. "Noooooo, you're not holding, why?" She wailed and started to lose her balance. "You reached there all by yourself." he reminded her.

"Can't believe he let go of me but I guess I did reach here all by myself, and I can get back up even if I fall. I have always healed from my wounds after falling..." she said to herself as she debated with her fears. With this self-assurance, she regained the balance she had lost momentarily. "Okay, let me try taking a turn as well." she thought, feeling braver. She did, and without a single fall she came peddling back with even greater joy knowing that she was always looked after even if it was from a distance, and as long as she had faith, she would be ok.

I learned a lot of things from that one experience of mine.

How the urge to go places drives us to get out of bed, how the feeling of finding our balance and making turns emboldens us to dream big, and how the trust that someone is there with you every step of the way protects us from our doubts and fears that lead us astray.

I wrote the above memory in the third person because I now view it not only from the perspective of my seven-year-old self but also from that of my dad and my current self. A grownup who is so happy to see their little one soar in happiness and confidence.

No matter how old you are, each one of us has an inner child in us who needs to be guided, assured, and celebrated.

If you are reading this, I want you to know that I am rooting for you. And I hope that by the end of this book, you will be truly rooting for yourself too.

"Our doubts are traitors,
and make us lose the good we oft might win,
by fearing to attempt."
—William Shakespeare

Even as a 10-year-old pondering over life in the backseat of her parents' car on a road trip, I conceived a dream of penning down the thoughts and epiphanies I was so amused by daily. As I never noted any of this down, I forgot a lot of these truths about life that I had always known. However, that set me up on a journey where every person I met, just through their interaction with me, nudged me to remember those long-forgotten secrets. (I know this retrospectively now, but being a sensitive person, the emotional vagaries of life hit me with a sharp intensity back then).

Although sensitive, I was always an optimistic person living moment to moment. How and when this person turned into an overwhelmed, frustrated, people-pleasing numb individual is hard to pinpoint. It's also true that losing my optimism —a core trait of mine pushed me to question life and what we have been told to find better answers I can rely on. My undying spirit made me want to understand life's circumstances and the chaos it puts us through, despite facing several failures and heartbreaks. I grew up to understand that I was not alone on this journey. Every human is a traveler paving their own path to uncovering the meaning of life to whatever extent they can in this lifetime. If you have found this book, it's time you uncover some deeper perspectives by reading this book as an honest conversation between two travelers —two friends. Please note that this book is not meant to push you to accept my understanding and insight as the one and only truth, rather it's intended to make you think for yourself and find the answers that you have always known at your core.

Two things about me I know for sure are that I love meaningful conversations and I care about the human condition deeply enough to get over my insecurities and fears to do what I can to help. I see these writings as a way to do so. Also, considering I am a seemingly extroverted introvert who would rather not talk constantly, this method of sharing my findings and love sits well with me.

I have written this book in a semi-informal conversational tone because that is what I want this book and all my books to be—an honest conversation that engages your mind and heart. So come along with me for this ride as our paths converge, making way for more laughs and memorable mental conversations to emerge.

# THE WHAT

# CHAPTER 1

# Define Unshakeable

What does 'being unshakeable' signify? Does it mean to never fall? Does it mean resilience? What is true resilience? Is it merely the ability to cope and get by? Or is it the drive to not just survive but thrive? Who do you first think of when you think about resilience? A sports person, an army veteran, some person you know? Did you think of yourself first? Why not? I know these are a lot of questions.

If someone just gave you an answer, it will probably stay in your brain for hours, days, or a few months. However, when your mind gets involved in solving the problem, the answer will sink deeper and probably stay there for a lifetime. That is how most people activate resilience. It takes a challenge or some pressure for us to reflect on where we are, who we are, and where we need to go, or else it's easy to fall into the trap of complaining about the mundane or disappointing aspects of life on auto-pilot. We go from taking things for granted when life is good to groveling for a change from disappointment and hoping for a miracle that will renew life again.

It reminds me of how we have a lackadaisical approach towards our health in general, not caring for it enough, only to sit and barter with God when we have fallen sick. We make all sorts of promises to care more and take better precautions the next time around, but repeat that same behavior, as it has subconsciously become our default. No wonder resilience is seen as the ability to bounce back after hardship, given we are always anticipating challenges based on our experiences in the past, thinking good times do not last. But... what if I tell you that's not what resilience is about? Bouncing back is only a cog in the grand machine of being unshakeable.

I am not just interrogating you but I also asked these questions to quite a few people. Here is what they had to say:

<u>The Engineer:</u> Ability to get back to the original shape.

<u>The Parenting Coach:</u> Not giving up when faced with negative or unexpected outcomes. Not letting go of our values and ideas when the going gets tougher. Taking the right action, even when no one is watching, whether or not it aligns with our selfish desires. Resilience is being flexible and mentally tough, preparing ourselves to confront obstacles in life with bravery, understanding, and a positive attitude, and ultimately becoming a compassionate leader.

<u>The Chartered accountant:</u> I think resilience for me is forgetting or moving past the problems, failures, and bad times by not dwelling upon them. Not getting into the spirals of why me? What could I have done differently or why did XYZ person do this to me? Believing that you can always have a fresh start is important too. Although difficult, believe that you can fail so often but still win eventually if you keep at it. Not taking failures too seriously and somehow mustering the courage to get up again and again, fully knowing and accepting that you will continue to keep failing in the future as well is key. I feel it's just an attitude, as anything that requires effort like exams, jobs, ratings, or

personal relationships doesn't come easy. You just have to decide to be resilient and come back stronger the next day.

<u>The Musician:</u> You never know when you will strike the right note and until you do, you just keep playing with passion and faith. Why? Because the melody you are creating is too beautiful to be marred by some bruises that come in the form of judgment and failure.

<u>The Sports person:</u> It's the mental toughness that bridges success and failure. If you can train and practice regularly, while maintaining a mental diet and exercising focus, you got it, whatever your goal is.

People have contested the definition of resilience, with each person giving it their own meaning. All the above statements are correct, but why is it so hard to follow? Why do we know it all but do very little of it? Why does it feel like something is missing?

Have you ever played with a bouncing ball? You smack it into the ground once and then it keeps bouncing up and down, eventually losing its energy and coming to a stop. Something similar happens to us humans. We have all heard

"What doesn't kill you makes you stronger" and "No pain, no gain" but more often than not, constant exposure to intense pain will wreck you. Many people put on a brave face and push through life's issues, but the never-ending stress just breaks their spirit down after a while. When you repeatedly find yourself in survival mode, it becomes hard to think straight or appreciate life. No wonder people in our societies are so grumpy and skeptical most of the time —the continuous wear and tear has worn them out. So, should our definition of being resilient really depend upon always experiencing pain?

Consider buildings and other infrastructure being wrecked by a catastrophic event like an earthquake. Is the best solution here only to plan the quick rescue and recovery or is it thoughtfully constructing infrastructure that is less prone to damage and more prone to save several lives?

Why do we wait for some event that is upsetting and uprooting to bounce higher and be better? Pain is a great agent of change but it also inherently carries chaos, and if we keep waiting to get beaten up so that we can get stronger, we will always see life as a struggle filled with bruises, bandages with some light-hearted good moments peppered in here and there. If bouncing back is not true resilience, then what is? True resilience is when the internal environment remains unaffected by external factors, allowing us to continue gathering momentum and facing challenges. Putting effort into developing your internal mental models paves the way for a path of least resistance.

Resilient people embody realistic optimism; the ability to focus on the bright side of a tough situation and acknowledge the challenging nature of it. They can look inward, analyze their own thoughts and feelings, and understand others' perspectives as well. And in moments of need, they do not shy away from reaching out to a close-knit group of friends for support and guidance. They ruminate less and optimize more because their self-esteem is delinked from external circumstances. Quite like a willow tree, they bend and adapt to change without breaking.

So, it would be fair to say that a modern definition of being unshakeable is 'advancing despite adversity' owing to the inner sense of self, vision, strength, and the external supportive systems in place from the start. When is this 'start'? Is it right before the challenge, afterward, or at birth? You sow the seeds of an unshakeable human, as soon as you realize the importance of taking charge of your own thoughts, emotions, and actions to build a strong and exciting future.

The mere thought of taking accountability for our life and its events scares the hell out of us. Ever since we were kids, making mistakes and owning up to them has been an unpleasant experience. Our brains learn to equate a mistake to being yelled at and humiliated, diminishing our self-worth and making it something to avoid at all costs as a safety measure against howling caregivers, teachers, or other authority figures. However, every mistake is a reflection point, not a shrinkage point where your self-worth is battered into oblivion.

People's reactions to your mistakes might make you feel you should just stick your head in the sand and never be seen again, but every mistake is simply feedback that you can use to build a better experienced version of yourself. Own your past mistakes so that your past mistakes do not own you. If you continue to deny accountability, you are escaping from the problem temporarily and burying the problem inside of you permanently. Whatever is inside of you is bound to make it outside at some point because there is only so much that one can hide.

Respect, courage, and humility are qualities you gain when you accept your follies, which are highly attractive traits that make people root for you. Without ownership of your mistakes, your inner guilt and shame will hold your worthiness hostage for longer than you think it will. Taking accountability, although embarrassing, is the difference between someone who is responsible and someone who isn't. Someone who can be trusted and someone who can't. Trust is one of the most precious things you can earn in this lifetime, especially in an increasingly distrustful world.

A Harvard Business Review study found that people in high-trust companies report 74% less stress, 106% more energy at work, 50% higher productivity, 13% fewer sick days, 76% more engagement, 29% more satisfaction with their lives, and 40% less burnout than those in low-trust companies.[1] Leaders who hold themselves accountable are more likely to inspire trust among their teams and inspire innovation.[2] Taking accountability has a profound impact on personal and professional success. Around 85% of workplace success is tied to emotional intelligence, of which accountability is a core component.[3] As you make the conscious decision to own your choices, it feels like the morning fog is lifting to reveal a clear path. The previous uncertainty that obscured your perspective fades away, and you feel a sense of stability replacing it.

*Responsibility without agency and accountability is drudgery.*

When you don't take accountability, you won't know where you went wrong and are, therefore, prone to repeating the same mistake. Accountability not only sharpens your focus, but it also builds an inner confidence that radiates outwards, drawing others into your orbit of reliability and trust.[3] Trust is what gets the ball rolling towards substantial change. In moments of doubt, follow the key quality of a sturdy tree—rooted firmly in your own integrity, even when the winds of uncertainty blow hardest. Be accountable to yourself to become valuable to yourself.

How do you do that? Most children are naturally quite confident and believe they can do anything, but they lack accountability and haven't found or polished their skills at that age. When they fail and record the critique of their loved ones as a disappointment, they start to believe that they are not good enough and they can't do anything right, and hence are not worthy of getting what they want. As a result, disempowering beliefs solidified even though it was just a matter of their unique set of skills not getting enough attention, time, or encouragement to be mastered. Parents are so busy trying to find in their own children the same qualities that their neighbors' or relatives' kids have that they completely miss out on the abilities that make their kids uniquely powerful. This may stem from the fear and the responsibility of seeing if their child is developing "normally" or not by comparing them to others.

Skill sets are not one size fits all. Everyone has unique ones. That is how and why we add value to each other's lives. To give and receive. If there were only people of a certain profession and skill set in the world, civilization would not exist. Because if everyone is a clone of the other, there is only supply but no demand. To ask a person to master every skill set under the sun is another unrealistic goose chase. The answer? Find your unique skill set, and master it so well that you know your worth and it gives you the confidence that naturally overflows into other areas of your life.

Take the initiative to learn and develop yourself. In today's fast-paced world, having a degree is not enough. The world is constantly evolving, and so should we. It's important to keep learning and developing ourselves to stay relevant and competitive. However, many people fall into the trap of complacency, thinking that what they already know is enough. They hide behind the shield of "I know", unwilling to challenge themselves and expand their knowledge and skills. But what we know is always just a small fraction of what is out there for us to learn. Don't wait to lose your job to upskill yourself. Start learning it today with enthusiasm so that you can get a promotion instead.

**Actionable point:** Make a list of strengths and weaknesses right now (at least 5). Note down where and how you want to apply your strengths more. Also, note down how you are going to improve your weaknesses and why it's important to do so.

| **Strengths** | | **Weaknesses** | | |
|---|---|---|---|---|
| *What is it?* | *Where/How are you going to apply them more?* | *What is it?* | *Why does improving this matter?* | *How do you want to improve it?* |
| | | | | |
| | | | | |
| | | | | |
| | | | | |

You are not as inadequate, lost, or confused as you think you are. If you direct your brain to the right questions, it will retrieve the right answers in tandem with your heart's intelligence. It might seem absurd for some to believe that the heart holds any connection to intelligence. We will discuss how in the upcoming chapters. Choose where you want to go, proactively start developing your skill set and supportive network of relationships that you know are in alignment with where you want to be, and start looking at challenges, big or small, as puzzles to solve. Most importantly, start. Start now because that is the only clay you can mold.

# CHAPTER 2

# Origins of Unshakeable Resilience

Even before the appearance of human beings, nature has been replete with examples of resilience. All our circumstances, limitations, and actions can make us feel as tiny as ants sometimes in a ridiculously overwhelming world... but do you know ants are as old as dinosaurs? [4,5] Although those mighty dinosaurs disappeared, ants are still here doing their job, serving their community, and getting satisfaction from it. Just like humans, ants are incredibly social creatures, with special structures and functions in their brains that allow them to cooperate and form strong bonds with their community. In fact, certain species of ants collaboratively cultivate and gather mushrooms as a source of food, and they can also lift 50 times their body weight.[4]

As tiny and unseen as you may sometimes feel, know that just like those tireless ants, your existence is serving an ecosystem. How well is it serving the ecosystem? That's up to you to decide. People migrate to different countries to find a better environment, but they also end up taking the toxic traits they picked up in the first place, inadvertently recreating the same environment they wanted to escape from. Environment is essential, yes, but it's incomplete without you. You must change to fit the new environment you wish to adapt and integrate into so that you become capable of adding value to that ecosystem. Most people get tired of managing and adding value to their own lives, so they fail to consider the bigger picture. But here is the thing: if you see yourself as being separate from everyone else, stuck in your own world, you shut out the support you might get from others. Being independent does not mean you can never seek help from anyone else in life. That is a faulty perception the modern world has created. It only isolates you further and makes you feel you must deal with everything in your life all by yourself. One brick does not build a house. You can be self-sufficient and still ask for help. Learning from others by asking for help is inevitable. Asking for help is not beneath you or above you, it's for you. All you can do is try.

Ever seen an elephant calf? Not only does the playful little creature have a funny arm growing out of its face, but it's also tasked with figuring out how to use it. It struggles to figure out how to use its trunk to pick up food, but it keeps trying until it succeeds. Similarly, human beings possess all sorts of strengths and talents that may appear insignificant until they become their most defining feature and biggest lifeline. Are you allowing yourself to find and master this gift, though?

Each one of us has been gifted a brain and some complementary DNA upon which our existence impinges. However, both remain shrouded in mystery, with much of their secrets yet to be revealed. Our biology classes have drilled into our brains that proteins are the building blocks of life. However, as much as 98 percent of our DNA does not code for proteins. So, what is most of the DNA really coding for? Many scientists believe that much of this "dark matter genome" comprises nonfunctional evolutionary leftovers that are simply tagging along.[6,7] We humans have approximately 86 billion neurons in our brains, woven together by about 100 trillion connections, or synapses.[8,9] It's a daunting task to understand the details of how those cells work, let alone how they come together to make up our sensory systems, our behavior, and our consciousness. So far, there is no evidence that there is one site for consciousness, which leads experts to believe that it's truly a collective neural effort. In this light, complaining about our limitations and what we have in our lives is quite redundant, as we do not even know the full potential of our brain and our genes. To become unshakeable, the key is not to gather motivation to bounce back, but to understand what we have been given —be it strengths or challenges, and why we have them. We all have the same equipment, but the way we use our faculties varies widely, and that makes all the difference.

What if, instead of viewing our strengths and challenges as separate entities to be analyzed and dissected, we saw them as interconnected pieces of a complex puzzle that made us who we are? Let me explain this with a short story.

Once in a land of rugged terrain and boundless beauty, there was a legendary mountain called the Peak of Echoes. Wildflowers of every color adorned the landscape. The summit of the mountain was shrouded in an ethereal mist as its peaks pierced through the clouds. People believed this mysterious mountaintop to be the dwelling of the wisest sage in the land. Three men, each bearing a unique gift and a common goal, set out to seek the sage's wisdom.

The first man, Lucas, was a skilled swimmer. His knowledge of water currents and ability to navigate even the most turbulent rivers was unmatched, but his lack of intellect often led him to overlook simple solutions.

The second man, Adrian, was a masterful engineer. He could design phenomenal structures with minimal resources, but his frail physique meant he struggled with the physical demands of their journey.

The third person, Vincent, had an acute hearing and could detect the faintest sounds from miles away. Tragically, an accident had rendered him paraplegic, confining him to a wheelchair, and disconnected him from others living a normal life.

Their journey led them to the roaring river called Woroshi which created a vast swirling barrier between them and the mountain. Neither man spoke to the other and each of them set out to find a solution for themselves. Lucas's unmatched swimming skills allowed him to glide through the water and cross it. Vincent could hear some fisher folk and boats in the distance, so he started moving his wheelchair in that direction. Adrian started building a makeshift bridge.

A few miles after crossing Woroshi, these three men encountered yet another majestic and glistening river called Sangam. This time, they shared their experience of crossing the River Woroshi with one another. Lucas proudly proclaimed that he just swam across the river, and it was no big deal. Adrian then questioned, were you not scared of the crocodiles known to patrol these rivers? Lucas had not even considered that possibility! Adrian narrated how he was just able to make the crossing, but it felt like the bridge could collapse at any moment.

Vincent pitched in, saying he wasn't sure if he would get lucky enough to find people with boats again to cross this river. The fear of being devoured by crocodiles gripped Lucas, while Adrian's heart raced at the thought of the bridge crumbling beneath their feet, leaving them stranded in the middle of the deep river. "You know, I've always preferred my encounters with wildlife to be on land," Lucas joked, trying to mask his unease. Vincent suggested they join forces and that he would be very interested to see how Adrian can build a bridge. Having unintentionally bonded over their troubles, the three men banded together.

Lucas, with his swimming prowess, dove right in, but quickly realized that the river's strong currents could be dangerous. He advised his companions on the safest point to cross.

However, the challenge of crossing the river loomed large. Adrian, using his engineering skills, proposed building a sturdy, makeshift bridge that could support Vincent's wheelchair. He guided Lucas, who did the heavy lifting and gathered materials from the surrounding wilderness.

As they began their construction, Vincent, with his extraordinary hearing, alerted them to the distant sound of a breaking tree, a warning of potential danger. This timely intervention allowed them to move their camp to safety and avoid a disastrous landslide.

As they hammered the final plank into place, a loud crack echoed through the valley, sending a jolt of panic through their veins. The bridge seemed shaky. With bated breath, they took their first steps, unsure if the bridge would hold their weight. Despite the panic, they completed building the bridge and successfully crossed the river. As they approached the mountain, they encountered paths riddled with hazards. Vincent's hearing became their greatest asset, as he could hear rockslides before they happened, or sense wild animals, guiding them through safer paths.

Their ascent was slow because of Vincent's condition, but Lucas and Adrian took turns carrying him on their backs. Vincent used his keen hearing to navigate them through dense fogs and treacherous terrain, where visibility was near zero. However, a wave of guilt washed over

Vincent, threatening to drown his spirits, but Lucas and Adrian rushed to his defense, showering him with gratitude and reminding him of the countless times his acute hearing had guided them through dangerous situations and brought them closer to their goal. They each had something to teach and learn from one another, and Vincent's belief that he was going to get to the mountaintop had inspired both of them profoundly and gave them the courage and inspiration to be more mindful and look out for opportunities.

Upon reaching the summit, they found the sage, who smiled knowingly. Turns out the sage had a secret. He confesses he is not a sage at all, but a sorcerer who orchestrated the entire journey for his own amusement and for the benefit of three men. "You already have everything you need, so just wake up." said the sorcerer. "Is this a joke?" Lucas exclaimed. Just as Adrian was about to say, "What do you really mean?" All three men opened their eyes to find themselves at their respective homes, with no one else around. It was only a dream, perhaps. However, this collective dream sequence had shown them that each person has a lot to offer, and when you find other people who can benefit from your skill, connect with them and don't carry any guilt or shame thinking you are not enough.

You may wonder…"You made me read this entire story to say, 'We already have everything we need?'" Seems like a bummer, but it's the greatest realization one can have to live this life in peace. We are not meant to live in isolation and be tangled up in fear. When you realize you have some pretty great strengths of your own that you can help others with and receive their support in return, you stop feeling like the world rests on your shoulders. "But no one supports me!"–We'll address this later. For now, just remember to always play to your strengths because if you try to copy and paste someone else's solution even though it does not match your gifts, you will slip, slide, and lose faith in yourself. Learn from one another, expand your capabilities, beliefs, and brotherhood, and you have successfully expanded your horizons.

You may be wondering… but Nidhi these are all just platitudes and la-la land stories, in reality, there is war, crime, hate, cheating, distrust, jealousy, and pain, which is too much for a person to take even if there are good moments here and there. Screw crossing the river, screw the mountain, let me just lie here! Ok, let us challenge that in the next chapter. Catch you there.

# CHAPTER 3

# Resilience Personified

Who does not love a good story? From bedtime tales to mythology to history, to fictional odysseys of books and movies, or even real-life events, news, and gossip, stories have influenced us throughout our lives. I caught up with 8 people who seemed to have interesting stories to share. Little did I know I would find not just an intriguing narrative but also a profound message of what keeps us going despite the ordeals we face.

**The Meaningful Space: Dysfunction Overcome by The Power of Love**

OBSERVER: Let us begin. Could you tell me a little about yourself?

SURAJ: From the start?

OBSERVER: Sure.

SURAJ: I was a shy and underappreciated kid born to a para-military father and a mother who is a self-made naturopathy healing doctor. They were like the contrast of day and night. I also have a younger brother.

OBSERVER: Parents tend to be our role models by default.

SURAJ: My father's job whisked us from one corner of India to another, so experiencing constant change and diverse cultures became a staple. This nomadic life mirrored my academic journey, as I found it confusing to be routinely uprooted just when I was finding my footing in any school. I had to repeat a couple of grades.

OBSERVER: Did you have any specific aspirations?

SURAJ: Amidst this whirlwind of relocations and readjustments, I wanted to join the nation's defense wing, as an Air Force pilot. I joined the NCC Naval wing, where I tasted the rigor of national-level camps and I also enjoyed the thrill of college basketball, secured by a sports quota.

OBSERVER: Sounds good. You achieved these notable opportunities, so did your confidence soar?

SURAJ: No, not at all.

OBSERVER: Oh. Why not?

SURAJ: Our upbringing was not good. Beneath the surface of these achievements, the cracks in my roots, i.e., my family's life, were deepening. Our home was a battleground, marked by my grandmother's tyranny over my mother, our echoing hunger waiting for my father's money orders, and the strange puzzle of having three sets of grandparents. The early years of my life oscillated between innocence and turmoil, with moments of happiness shadowed by nights filled with fear and violence.

We were more structured and disciplined not by choice but by compulsion to avoid conflicts between parents. The turning point came when my mother, faced with the ultimatum of death or departure, carved out a new beginning for us. Her decision to leave with my father marked the end of one chapter and the start of another—filled with its own set of nightmares. My father's battles with alcohol, the dark cloud of domestic abuse, and the unsettling attention from his so-called friends towards my mother were the monsters of my childhood tales. All this affected us. My brother became an extrovert to hide from all this and forget the pain, and I became an introvert in 1st standard itself.

OBSERVER: That is quite a lot for one to handle on their own. Was it better because you moved around from city to city?

SURAJ: As we moved, the challenges morphed but never dissipated. Discrimination as "Madrasi" greeted us, not because of who we were but because of where we came from. People assumed my personality based on my skin color and accused me of frequent mischief. I was an easy scapegoat. What I realize now is that people everywhere have similar fears presenting as different insecurities based on their experiences. Back then, however, trusting people became an impossible task and so there were no friendships that I could lean on as well. I took a break year as we had no money for schooling and mom had just started work to fill our tummies.

OBSERVER: What did you do to get out of that situation?

SURAJ: At that young age, I did not know what I could do. Inspired by the movies of many actors in Hindi cinema, like Amitabh Bachchan,

Govinda, Akshay Kumar, and Anil Kapoor, I asked my mother to let me go. I still remember telling her I would survive on my own and would come to meet her someday. She, being a mother, took a chance for our future together, no matter what. One of my best memories was when I bunked on the first day of joining a new school. My mother could not believe it and the expression she had on her face was something beyond words. For her, that moment was me being a kid and rebelling normally, even after all the abnormal situations we had been in.

OBSERVER: Did you become bitter towards people and life after being in such difficult circumstances?

SURAJ: I rebelled in my own ways as a child, but then felt bad about heading down the same dark path that I saw my loved ones attempting to take. My father's disownment, the societal shame, physical abuse, and the breakdown of my first marriage under the weight of betrayal—each event felt like it was crafted to crush my spirit and confidence in ways I could not fathom. Every subsequent event seemed to carry more reason for me to become an inconsiderate and ruthless person. Somehow, I did not become bitter but just extremely cautious of what people think. It seemed like keeping quiet and hiding away from any sort of attention was the best option in life. Ending my life would only create more pain and suffering for the ones I love.

OBSERVER: How did you find the strength to keep going with life?

SURAJ: I was against marriages as I did not want my family saga to spill over to the next generation, but under pressure from my mom I got married but was cheated upon. The deceit and pain I experienced in that marriage left me all alone, with no support from my family. That was the final nail in the coffin of my past, and I decided that no other person should experience what I had experienced. I changed jobs and cities, found a new environment, and, more importantly, found a wonderful woman who could be my life partner and help me build a more loving home. The birth of my son, after several failed IVF attempts, was nothing short of a miracle and was all the hope and strength I needed to be stronger. When I held him for the first time, I was reminded of my own vulnerabilities and it was on that day that I vowed to end the legacy of suffering in my family.

Now, when I look back at my life, I realize that my strength lies not in the absence of fear but in the courage to face it head-on. Despite the scars of my battles, even in the darkest of times, there was light—a light that guided me toward a future where love and happiness are not just fleeting moments of wishful thinking but the very essence of our existence.

OBSERVER: What is your vision for your future now?

SURAJ: I cannot change this generation, but at least the next one should have sensible, compassionate, disciplined, resilient, and creative leaders who can help each other and make this society a better place. And I feel parents are the best people who nurture those young minds towards a growth mindset at an early age. As they are the closest role models to kids, they are the coaches who can cultivate emotional intelligence in their kids.

Normally, a new dad would feel happy holding his newborn. I, however, had mixed feelings, because a major chunk of fear from all that happened was still stuck in my chest. As I held him, I saw a montage of painful memories; mom holding a knife, being beaten up on the road, dad's violence, him begging us to stay, lady inappropriately touching me, my ex-wife cheating on me. Despite this waking nightmare, I fully awakened the protector in me when I saw the miracle I was holding. It was this profound moment that gave birth to a community dedicated to nurturing the next generation with sensitivity, resilience, and leadership as core values. And that's how The Meaningful Space Community was born.

My father is still with us. Everything is normal. My parents still fight. They are normal fights, but it will take time and inner healing to patch up with him mentally. I do not speak to him for my sake, but the birth of my son changed him. It's good that he is a much better grandfather than he was a father.

OBSERVER: After all this, who are you now?

SURAJ: I transformed from being a mess to an individual who accepted his life's experiences to become an awesome father, caring husband, responsible son, brother, and coach with a purpose.

OBSERVER: Thank you, Suraj.

*Right now, we still see communication breaking down in families because of a lack of trust, love, and respect between parents and their kids and between parents themselves. Because of this, the child, regardless of gender and age, becomes susceptible to abuse within and outside the family. Suraj is a wonderful example of how one can break his/her generational trauma and create a safe and beautiful environment for his child. Now not only is his child thriving, but he is also helping other parents create this deep bond and shape their kid's life holistically. However, it's not enough for one father to undergo this change; it's every parent's duty to educate themselves on how they can nurture their little ones and condition them for success instead of shame from a tender age.*

## Blessings in disguise: Escaping life-threatening experiences

*"Never let your schooling interfere with your education,"–Mark Twain*

OBSERVER: Miracles hit when you least expect them. I think you would agree.

DHARANIDHARAN: Definitely, miracles happen. They have happened to me and I cannot imagine where I would be without them.

OBSERVER: What has been the biggest miracle you have experienced in your life?

DHARANIDHARAN: It was December 26, 2004, a day after Christmas. We were in Chennai that day. My family and I had an exciting plan of going to the beach since it was a Sunday. My winter vacation was almost ending, and I wanted to make the most of it before school started, as I do not have a beach in my hometown. So, as a kid, having a Sunday picnic at Marina Beach in Chennai was a very regular and cherished event for me. I was up the night before, making several plans out of excitement. What I would wear, what I would do, who I would meet, and what I should take with me. However, because of staying up so late, I ended up oversleeping the next morning, and the entire plan was now delayed. Everyone was complaining about missing the pleasant weather and how it would take more time now to get there. I was already so upset about waking up late and everyone's taunts were only making me feel worse. It was as if I always missed out on all the things I looked forward to.

OBSERVER: You could still go, albeit a little late, so what happened next?

DHARANIDHARAN: I was getting ready when I suddenly heard sirens and screams. It was coming from the TV. As I ran into the hall to see what the commotion was all about, I was hit by shockingly upsetting news. It turned out that the Great Indian Ocean Tsunami had severely damaged the coasts of South and Southeast Asia. Had we gone to the beach as we had planned before, our lives would have been at stake. We then realized how lucky we were. Amidst all that suffering, we were fortunate enough to survive. I would certainly consider my life a Christmas gift, though I am not a religious person. Every year between Christmas and the New Year, I find a quiet moment to pay tribute to the countless lives that were lost in the merciless tsunami and the irreparable damage that was done to the global economy.

OBSERVER: Do you value your life more when you remember that event?

DHARANIDHARAN: I am incredibly grateful for being blessed with this life, even though there are many times when it gets really difficult to carry on and the world seems to close in on you.

OBSERVER: Could you please share an instance where it all seemed to go haywire, and what you got out of that situation?

DHARANIDHARAN: Ok, let us rewind back to the year 2007 for that. I was a kid with a terrible throat. It was not just a cold; it was more like a big battle that lasted for years. I would puke heavily almost every single day. My parents tried everything at home to avoid a scary surgery. But nothing worked. They did that because I'd already had enough surgeries, including major brain surgeries. The first one was done when I was just 7 days old. Eventually, we had to go to a big hospital in Chennai. What we thought would be a quick procedure, wasn't. The recovery was tough. After the surgery, I was weak. I couldn't even swallow a sip of water for months, and I missed a lot of school. But my mom helped me get notes from friends. The midterm exams were fast approaching, and I had to catch up. I studied really, really hard. Even though I was still weak, I wanted to do more than just pass. And I did—I got top grades in everything! (A whopping 100% in every single subject of that exam.)

OBSERVER: Life can take away something to give you something else. It does not seem to be fair, though. What do you think?

DHARANIDHARAN: There was a lot more that was taken away after that as well. Losing my father at a young age, getting sidetracked from the profession of my choice at the time (chartered accountant), not being able to graduate, and so on, but...

OBSERVER: But?

DHARANIDHARAN: The amazing experiences in life and the community of people I would meet after that were something I did not foresee. My loving mother taught me that there is more to life than just schoolwork. She encouraged me to engage in day-to-day affairs and other extra-curricular activities for fun. So, despite the several headaches, hurt, tears, and nightmares, I am still here learning and growing every day. It was the sense of comradery that was missing my whole life even though I was yearning for it.

Feeling like I was the odd one out was not new to me. I was picked on because of my squeaky voice in school and faced linguistic intolerance and supremacy, which disconnected me from my peers. Because I was innately curious, I would ask a ton of questions in class, which not only annoyed the students but even the teachers. Although they later admitted to being more thorough in their preparation because of me. So being authentic came at a price for me, but that is exactly what has made me stand out and be memorable, so I would not trade that in for people pleasing. Where there was only competition before, now I am seeing more avenues of collaboration.

OBSERVER: Was there something you learned about life from those painful experiences?

DHARANIDHARAN: This wasn't just about school. It was about learning something bigger. Success isn't about how many hours you study or how many resources you have. It's about how committed you are to something. Even if the odds seem to be against you, you still show up and do what you planned to do. Real winners keep going, no matter how hard it gets. I was a lost teen, feeling isolated from the world around me because I could not communicate the way they wanted me to. Language should never be a barrier to genuine connection and progress. No amount of bullying or discrimination could stop me from becoming a polyglot today who teaches multiple languages to aspiring students so that they can bridge the gap in their lives. That squeaky-voiced guy can now speak his mind with courage and handle life better than the ones who tried to pin him down.

OBSERVER: So, is life an easy ride now?

DHARANIDHARAN: Life still has its difficulties, but the good part is that I am calmer and more confident now, which makes even the challenges manageable with more ease. The more turbulent I was the more turbulent life used to get, which is not there anymore.

OBSERVER: Thank you for sharing, Dharanidharan.

*Life is too precious for us to just look at the imperfections and throw it away. If you are here reading this, there is a purpose for you to discover and create the experiences you want to live. You are alive for a reason, not just because some random sperm made it into an egg. Out of the millions of variants you could be, you have a unique personality for a specific purpose. Nobody else can truly walk in your shoes, so own every moment, even if it feels difficult at first. By not compromising on his values, his passions, and his idiosyncrasies, Dharanidharan not only stands out of the crowd but also inspires it. We live in a hyper-connected world, yet people have never felt lonelier because of the lack of honest conversations and the initiative to reach out to people by learning a new language. Rather than letting language become another 'us vs them' ploy that creates societal intolerance, let it be a channel for us to expand the potential of our brains and create meaningful connections.*

## The Arrow of Life: From being disabled to enabling several others

OBSERVER: Where are you from, Gajendra?

GAJENDRA: Ma'am, I am from the mountains. I was born in a village called Pauri Garhwal near Rishikesh, surrounded by trees, rivers, and Himalayan valleys.

OBSERVER: You have lived two lives in one, don't you think?

GAJENDRA: Growing up, I lived with my family of 9 members in a hut that had a majestic view of nature. The lush nature sustained us and gave us fruits to enjoy, but I never thought it would also give me the biggest challenge in my life. It was the year 2009; I had completed my Bachelor's degree in Journalism from Lovely Professional University in Punjab and was aspiring for a well-paying job. I was up on a tall tree, collecting fruits for my family, lost in my own world, when my foot slipped and life as I knew it ended. My spine was crushed at the C5-C6 level, causing paralysis in my arms and legs. I was now a quadriplegic. Besides not being able to control my limbs, I lost all control of my bowel and bladder movements as well. I could not move. Just stuck on the bed lying like a limb vegetable. From sprinting up trees and mountains to my body completely shutting down to me learning how to reboot it and teach it a new of living...it has been quite a journey.

OBSERVER: The spine is the body's primary support system that keeps us upright. When your own body could not support you, did you still find support?

GAJENDRA: The entire village showed up for me to support me when I fell and broke my neck. Being situated high up in the mountains, it was not an easy task to transport me to the nearest hospital. There was no ambulance, nothing. The shock of the event and the excruciating pain emanating from my body were so intense that I was not aware of who was around me and what was really happening. In that state, people took me from one hospital to another, as some hospitals refused help and some stated that there was nothing they could do for me. One year passed by and there was still no solution in sight, so I returned to my hut and waited to die.

My younger brother and parents did everything they could to support me with what they had and keep me alive. My arms were like sticks and my cot was my bathroom. By some fortunate turn of events, a rafting guide by the name of Kim Hartlin came to the village and saw my plight. At that moment, I could only ask him for one thing–poison. I had given up hope, and I just wanted to end it all. But Kim was determined. He brought me down from the mountain and helped me get surgery for my bedsores. Friends carried my cot down the mountain as I lay there, terrified of another fall. What more could I lose?

OBSERVER: Could you get treatment for your spinal injury as well?

GAJENDRA: With the help of angelic souls like Kim, I ended up at the Indian Spinal Injuries Center in Delhi, where I had my first taste of therapy, and saw the sunshine after three years of lying limp in a room. It was at that moment that some hope arose inside of me, and I felt like I had found myself in a new life. In this new set of circumstances that I found myself in, I decided to grow as a person. I did my exercises and started to become active and more confident. Seeing the progress in recovery, some were happy and inspired, but many also felt disheartened by their slow progress when they compared themselves to me. They sent me back home, leaving me feeling directionless and in the dark again.

OBSERVER: I suppose an individual can take the success of another as either inspiration or competition, depending on their perception. So, you continued to do your exercises at home?

GAJENDRA: Yes, I did what I could at home, but movement was still limited because of the small space and mountainous terrain. I ended up dislocating my hip as well, and with the help of Meera Swami, I received treatment at Fortis Hospital. It was here that I met Raman sir, who informed me about a group called ESCIP–Empowering Spinal Cord Injured Persons. I returned home, but Kim once again encouraged me to become a more functional and independent human, despite being a quadriplegic. So, in October 2013, hoping to empower myself, I arrived at ESCIP, where I found some solace in friends with similar experiences. When I arrived at ESCIP, I depended completely on my brother. Then life gifted me with another angel called

Jonathan Sigworth. Jonathan was the first quadriplegic I met who was independent in a wheelchair. He had gotten injured eight years ago in India after he fell off a cliff from a height of 70ft.

OBSERVER: Did you feel upset that someone who also was in the same circumstance as you are now is independent and quite mobile in life? Similar to how others have felt seeing your progress.

GAJENDRA: For me, it was an inspiration. He was a great example of what's possible for me next, the goal of functionality and fitness that I can work towards. Upon seeing the poor healthcare support and quality of life of quadriplegics in India, he was inspired to help. He was not only my friend, but he also became my peer mentor, sharing the skills he learned in the US.

OBSERVER: You went from asking for poison to inspiring others to live a happy, fit, and healthy life. What changed inside you?

GAJENDRA: I watched Jonathan maneuver the wheelchair with ease and felt courageous but I just could not believe how I could fall again, and again, and again, without getting hurt. It wasn't until I tried it myself that I realized I could do it if I allowed myself to unlearn, learn, and grow. I am happy that I have always been able to grasp new things quickly. I recognize that about myself. This recognition has boosted my spirit to learn new skills and tricks, do wheelies, and play rugby. Feeling that enthusiasm for learning and becoming better at being myself, I began going out with friends and socializing more. All the while sharing what I had learned with many of my new friends. I wanted to share this belief and knowledge of what is possible with other differently-abled people who were looking for hope. So, I started a Facebook page to share the useful skills, stories, and online resources that had helped me on my journey. The page now has 18K followers.

I worked as a peer mentor myself at the ESCIP House for a while. Now I work at a company in Gurugram to support my livelihood and I am trying my best to live a fulfilling life. To support that spirit in me that has kept me going, I took part in sports. I won a gold medal at the national Paralympics 100M backstroke swimming competition in 2024. Since 5th grade I was interested in the game of shooting, however, I could not take up sports like this because of financial constraints. I watched a lot of Mahabharata growing up, in which Lord Arjuna was the epitome of focus, seeing nothing but the intended target. The exhilaration you feel when your focus and entire body are aligned with the target is unmatchable. I now have a dream of representing India in Archery on the global stage.

OBSERVER: What is the secret behind your bright smile?

GAJENDRA: After all the struggles, my family's hope was that I recover completely. I have recovered and am still recovering more and more every day because of that spirit in me that keeps guiding me to the right sources. If I had given up hope, I would have gone back and deteriorated in my room not seeing the light of the day again, not knowing what and all is truly possible and available to me in the world. My home is a very peaceful, serene, and spiritual place. I have seen the pain but also the beauty in this world, coexisting side by side.

I am reminded of Shree Krishna ji words, he says "The person who knows the illusion and the truth of the world never gets disappointed and disheartened, one day or the other everyone must leave the illusion of this world behind, therefore, whatever time a person has, he must use it to keep doing good deeds and always remain happy. Not everyone gets this human birth and journey."

OBSERVER: What do you want people to know?

GAJENDRA: So, I want to echo those profound words that have helped me. I want to say nothing is permanent and always move forward, achieve your life goals, believe in yourself, and be happy. I have learned the following in life:

- We can move forward in life only when we understand our strengths.
- Whatever skill you have, use it according to time, after some time everything will be destroyed.
- Every moment of life is precious. Use it and live it well.
- The world talks a lot of nonsense, but how many mouths will you go around trying to shut? When you achieve success, they will automatically get silenced, so keep going.

OBSERVER: Thank you very much, Gajendra.

*As long as one's spirit is alive and joyous, even the broken body will learn to mend itself from within and soar to greater heights than before. Do your best and leave the rest. The more you beat yourself up for your past mistakes or those of others, the less of you there is to truly experience life the way you would like to. Your power is yours alone, and your spirit can fall from the highest mountain and still stay uncrushed because of its hunger to learn, inspire, and embark on an adventure. Humility grounds you and lays the foundation for an even more breathtaking rise into the skies.*

## To be or not to be? The power of choice and what it costs when you don't use it.

*"We have been in a lot of fear. In childhood, we believed we could be anyone. But as we grew up, we forgot that confidence and compared ourselves with the environment. A one where everyone was moving in a structured manner, following set rules, and being guided by mediocrity. That caused us to forget our greatest power, the power to be receptive."–Pinaki Mandal*

OBSERVER: Do you think your past has a deep hold over who you are today?

PINAKI: I remember a lot from my childhood. Currently in my thirties, I try to fall back into nostalgia, trying to figure out why I am like I am. Life is a meaningful journey for those who think so, but I kept it a choiceless journey for a long time. I didn't wish to choose my subjects or majors. I took chemical engineering just because I scored well in chemistry, even though I was getting better colleges for architecture and math. Undergrad was a great time; it was the first time I felt so free, but as time went by; it felt suffocating. When I joined, I was never in the mode of getting a degree or job; I just went through it as the environment took me. I fared well in my first year, then I got mixed up with a fairly 'tamasic' group of people and engaged my later years in gaming and partying. This nature stuck with me.

OBSERVER: How did that nature stick with you?

PINAKI: I lost interest in pursuing any job and was more inclined towards a semi-comfortable lifestyle. I didn't go for any job interviews after undergrad because I never decided to work. So, I took on the challenge of completing an MBA, which I started enthusiastically. I had several ideas and was interested in starting something of my own by the end of the first year. But then I again fell back to my lazy nature, shifted to comfort, and completely lost interest in life as a pursuit. My pursuits had more to do with exploring novel content and slacking. My parents never pressured me for a job until my dad came close to retirement. That was my second year in the MBA program, and he said that I should start being responsible for the sake of the family. That hit hard. I was a Mustang and never rode with the group. Now I had to carry a load; that seemed next to impossible in my subconscious. I felt I was part of a bandwagon, and that led me to feel that whatever you may do in life, you can't change it, so what is the use of doing anything? I started playing the victim card.

OBSERVER: Did you sabotage yourself to stay a victim? If so, give us an example.

PINAKI: This feeling of pursuing a repetitive job really irked me. I went for over 50 interviews with the same attitude and didn't get accepted. I either argued with the interviewer or didn't respond authentically. And the funny thing was that I felt these failures were nothing. I gave up learning from them. That was when my emotions started fluctuating, but my outer cover showed no such signs. I didn't cry or laugh; I partied with friends like a rag doll. These interviews were arranged by the college; they still called companies about 2 months after the session ended. But I quit giving interviews midway and came back home. Here, I got into a company through my father's reference. Now miraculously, my father did not retire and was given the opportunity to continue working because of his service record. He had a prominent position and was hardworking, so he got me into one of his vendor companies.

See the paradox here; I took so much pressure and killed my emotional well-being because of what my father said about getting a job, and now here I was working for a company through his reference. Had he not been where he was, what would I have done? Anyway, I have been working for over 8 years now and have explored many fronts. I have worked with defense forces, government agencies, and international syndicates and have switched roles from product manager to sales to marketing and now to pre-sales consultant. All of this has taught me that a job is not my cup of tea, because no matter how good I am, my surroundings just don't accept it, and that makes me feel guilty. But I still put in my best.

OBSERVER: Did you consider starting a business then to know if that's your flavor of tea?

PINAKI: Business is what brings true transformation to life. I have had several business ideas and have also been on the verge of starting a few. However, I settled on being a coach for mindfulness and emotional wellbeing. In the meantime, I got married. That is another story.

OBSERVER: Tell us, did getting married affect the pursuit of your aspirations?

PINAKI: I was persuaded into marriage by my parents (again), who said "Who will you talk to when we are not around?" They saw I had become too silent in my approach. So, after I agreed, they started showing me profiles of urban girls who were working. I simply couldn't say yes to even meeting them. There was a strong resistance to it within me. Then a family friend sent a profile of a girl from the suburbs who was still completing her education. I thought, "What the heck? Let's at least talk." Now she is my wife, and we have the cutest kid on the block.

Life post-marriage was also a headache sometimes. Mostly because I was unsure of how to manage the communication between my wife and parents. There are so many inconsistencies in the communication flow that now I have become a master at averting both of them! Just kidding, but once there was a time when I was living apart from my wife and planned to leave my parents' house and settle somewhere nearby and bring back my wife. That's when I met my mentor and understood how I was ruining my mood and relationships at the same time. I kept running away and escaping it all whenever it came up, so the situation kept showing up. It pushed me to understand what it means to be a powerful human being, the simple ways in which energy flows through our thoughts, and the very nature of our minds. That was when I took accountability and started influencing my situation. I encouraged my family to come together again. Settled back at my parent's place with my wife and kid.

OBSERVER: Why did you keep your life as a choiceless journey for so long?

PINAKI: So, I used to feel if I remained choiceless, I would not have any burdens in life. It never came true. I was always thrown into situations where I had to make choices. There was a time when I was a prefect in school and had to choose another female prefect. Being uncomfortable, I delayed the process, so the teacher made me listen to the candidates and choose in front of the entire class. It felt like a courtroom where I was the judge, but I felt my choices could make or break someone's social standing. I made a good judgment then, but I quit being prefect the following year.

OBSERVER: What do you think life has tried to show you so far?

PINAKI: Choices hold the weight of responsibility along with them, but I kid you not, you need to choose; do not leave things to chance, because if you do not seek challenges, your mind will make things challenging around you to keep you at your will's end. Mindfulness is essential for such situations, as is understanding your patterns. Most of the time, we are in the way of our success and happiness. After learning it the hard way, I try to teach others how to recover from anxiety and stress. This not only assists others but also deepens my self-awareness.

OBSERVER: Thank you, Pinaki.

*The biggest tool a person has in this life is the ability to make a choice. Even if you have to live through its consequences, down the road, you will be very happy about making your own choices because they led you on your unique journey of life. When you give away your power of choice to the people and circumstances around you, you give away the force needed to shape your destiny. Hence, you simply end up forcing someone else's expectations on yourself and subscribe to living like an imposter, never truly feeling fulfilled because of a life half-lived. So, choose with courage.*

# You've come this far, what are two more steps?

*"What are two more steps to being free?"–Dhara*

OBSERVER: Taking the first step, can you tell us a little bit about yourself?

DHARA: For the world, I am a '77-born software engineer, learner, trainer, writer, and dancer by passion. But who am I to myself? Well, that is the ever-unfolding mystery, isn't it? The good thing is I am solving more and more of that puzzle every day.

OBSERVER: What are your roots? Where do you come from?

DHARA: I am from Hyderabad, India. I come from an orthodox patriarchal family that did not think educating the girl child was important, as she was created to just look after the household business, as per their belief. My roots extend to the Kuchipudi dance form, which originated in Andhra Pradesh and is one of the classical dances of India. Dance is not just a cherished heritage for me, but it's also food for my soul. My mother is an explorer. She has lived in several places and especially enjoys the Bengali culture and language. I have taken after her in that essence. Just like her, I love to learn new things and keep expanding my experiences in life. The only difference is she did not get the opportunity to do so, but somehow, I created those opportunities for myself and forged ahead to take care of her and my siblings. She did not know how to read and write in English, so I taught her, and I still continue to teach her the things I am learning. That is how we bond.

OBSERVER: What about your father? Why did you have to take up responsibility at a young age?

DHARA: I love my father. However, I have had a very difficult relationship with him. Even though he was supposed to be the protector of the family, the repeated domestic violence inflicted by him on my mother, me, and my siblings created a very unstable and unsafe environment. I saw my father hurting the people who loved him in fits of rage, which shattered my trust to the bone. I had to search for my independence and way out of the household, not just for me, but also for my siblings. However, the guilt of not being able to save my mom kept eating away at me. I could never stand up to him then. Just the thought of standing up to him itself was daunting enough to make me giddy. My mother had accepted her fate as his victim. That was my first wound by a masculine figure that became a core memory.

OBSERVER: Most of the violence against women is perpetuated by known members of the family.

DHARA: When I was young, about 13 years of age, I have a memory of playing in the backyard, when suddenly my maternal grandfather reprimanded me and took me into a room. The next thing I knew I was being sexually abused, and I could not even understand what it was and what was happening to me. I just know I felt completely destroyed, sick to my stomach, lost, confused, and hurt, with no one to protect me. I developed a bleeding disorder after that experience, which lasted several years. What do you do when the same people who are meant to protect and nurture you make you bleed in ways you could have never imagined?

There was so much shame and pain within me. I did not know what to do with it. I saw the plight of my mother and the rage of my father and decided to bury that memory and all the devastation it created in the core of my being.

Little did I know I was harboring a volcano inside of me, because where else would all that anger go? The only way I knew to protect myself was to close off my body, my heart, and my femininity, become a provider, and a breadwinner, trust no one, protect myself, and adopt a more masculine stance. I was a deer in all my relationships just running for her life, so I became the lion, at least professionally, by taking initiative, doling out critique like a judge, and pushing my team to get the best work out of them.

OBSERVER: Did those jarring wounds hinder you from finding love?

DHARA: I would not let anyone come within a 1-meter radius of me. Forget touching or hugging someone. The universe, though... had other plans. It sent me a kindred soul who could somehow break down my iron walls with his compassion and care. The thoughtful, gentle yet protective side of him had over time reawakened the women in me, building trust and opening my sealed-off heart little by little. I vividly remember the day he politely asked me if he could hold my hand. As I allowed him to do so, I could not believe how safe and reassuring a touch had felt in decades. However, our paths forked in different directions, with an unsaid promise of always being there for each other.

I got married to a quiet man, a good person, but an emotionally unavailable husband. Once again, I took on the role of the provider. To make my husband feel more masculine in our relationship, I would give him control over our finances, including my salary. I found someone emotionally unavailable because I was emotionally unavailable myself. I used to believe crying was for losers, so I locked it up in a vault inside me and threw away the key.

OBSERVER: Despite what you have been through, you have been there for others throughout your life, but have you ever lived for yourself?

DHARA: The day after the 2014 New Year, I found myself admitted to the hospital in a critical condition. I was sure this was the end until I felt someone gently grip my hand, and of all the feelings coursing through my body, I remembered my love for my divine god Shiva and his (and mine) penchant for dance. Since that moment, I made up my mind to recover, stay alive, and live for myself, expressing myself through dance. I awakened my classical dancer roots under the mentorship of Bala Tripura Sundari and began to heal as I found an anchor — dance. Life then took its own turns, and in Oct 2022, I left my full-time software career, as I felt stuck in life and wanted to live a bit differently. My personal vow was that if I couldn't figure out how to get unstuck, I would not live beyond the Dasara festival in September 2023.

I did a lot of small and big freelancing jobs. I embarked on some personal development programs and liked them. Yet, life always seemed like a war, and no matter what I did, I could not fill the void within. Yet something in me pushed me to re-attend the programs and give it my best shot. Along with the encouragement of my dear friend who had also joined the program, I worked towards making this sort of self-care a habit, which has always been alien to me. I knew I had to work on myself and needed a lot of help. When I did, even though it felt immensely tough, I could see breakthroughs that started out small and got bigger and bigger as I healed and opened up my heart. For the first time, I felt my father cared for me. I started connecting with people, attending a community event where I gave and received so many hugs it might as well be in the Guinness Book of records, I significantly progressed in my full-time job, negotiated with my boss effectively, and fulfilled all the things on my 2024 vision board in the first 4 months itself.

Yet, I still have my days of triggers and panic, but instead of spiraling and getting on a myriad of medications–I am healing, and that makes a world of difference. I am pursuing my interests and bringing my focus back to my well-being with the support and encouragement of my mentors, friends, and the divine.

OBSERVER: The festival of Dasara symbolizes the quelling of darkness by the light, but you planned to extinguish your own light because of conflicts in and around you. Still, the light trickled down to find and illuminate the life within you with the help of many little diyas (lamps) in the form of soulmates, mentors, poetry, dance, and a spiritual calling. So, by the end of this conversation, if I ask you "Who are you to yourself?" —what would you say?

DHARA: Now I am my best critic and working on being my best friend because these two roles will keep you going regardless of time, space, and mood and there is no one better than ourselves to fill these shoes.

**In just two more steps, maybe**
*While,*
*Avoiding the boats that keep rocking*
*Disowning the self that appear shocking*
*Rejecting the dreams that seem fading*
*Refusing faith in the time of fear mongering*

*There could be a sudden twist,*
*Why not walk past it*
*In just two more steps, maybe*

*The twist that's full of disappointment*
*Life that goes on devoid of contentment*
*Unable to carry the burden of sadness*
*Reckoning force, driving one to madness*
*Life certainly seems unliveable*
*Resting in peace seems inevitable*

*Looking for what's worth in all of this*

*A change seems to be hidden in this challenge*
*In just two more steps, maybe*

*How about I find a kind heart that listens*
*Someone who knows how it matters*
*While walking on a thorny path of the darkest*
*night*
*Silver lining that is seen at the ecliptic sight*
*Scent of hope that comes along with breeze*
*Warmth of the hand that comes to ease*

*Reaching for the arms that ultimately hold me*
*In just two more shaky steps taken*
*Telling me, everything is gonna be okay, trust*
*me!*

*Tears filled eyes, look up to see the angel*
*Only to realise*
*It's the grown up and healed, the future 'me!'*

*—  Ananya Dhara Vahini*

*A lot of us consume ourselves and extinguish*
*our light in trying to live for everyone except*
*ourselves. When we say we want to help people*

*we often forget that we are part of the collective we call people. So it is our first and foremost duty to adore, respect, and stand up for ourselves as you cannot pour for others from an empty cup. You may have found a lot of pain, heartbreak, and anger in life but let that not tame your desire to be free, loved, and happy. Your insecurities and trauma may try to crack you apart but piece them together by accepting and loving that part of you that feels that way. Give to yourself what you seek from others. Your inner child looks at you for assurance, love, and acceptance as you are their biggest protector. When you abandon that child as an adult, regardless of your age you become the child that feels abandoned by the universe. If that's so, what are two more steps of acceptance and love to be free?*

## Hakuna Matata: Sailing the world with an indomitable spirit

*Your children are not your children.*

*They are the sons and daughters of life's longing for itself.*

*They come through you, but not from you,*

*And though they are with you, yet they belong not to you.*

*You may give them your love, but not your thoughts,*

*For they have their own thoughts.*

*You are the bows from which your children as living arrows are sent forth.*

*–   Khalil Gibran*

*Born during the apartheid era in South Africa, the wondrous mind and rebellious spirit of a young 21-year-old Titch kept her toes ready to explore more than the injustice she saw around her. The whole world was her oyster, and there was an adventure waiting for her everywhere she went. When her plans of joining a group of friends to travel up through Africa, across the Middle East to finally land up in*

*Australia fell through, she boarded a ship with her friend Cindy and traveled to Southampton and on to London.*

OBSERVER: What kind of ship was it? Where did you go upon landing?

TITCH: It was a huge South African Cruise liner that would normally carry over a thousand passengers, but this time the ship was very empty, because of the six-day war and the escalating fuel prices. There were only 280 passengers, and we were in the first class. "If you mix with the cabin crew, the stewards, and the servers, you'll never get invited to the captain's cocktail party."–we were told. We didn't listen. We mingled with everyone and were well-known on the ship. Hearing our laughter with a sizeable group of friends, the captain of the ship walked up to us, introduced himself, and invited us to the cocktail party. So, for the Captain's Cocktail dinner, we got our stilettos on though we could not walk in them because of the swaying motions of the ship deck! In those days, all vessels that crossed the equator would have a party. A "We made it" celebration. We arrived at Southampton 21 days later. By the time we arrived, it was a biting cold winter, and we hardly saw anyone step foot outside. I ended up staying in a basement flat in Earls Court. It's where I learned not to be shy of my body because there was one bathroom and 21 people in the flat. You could have your bath running and someone would walk right in and pee!

OBSERVER: Did you move out soon after? Where did you end up working?

TITCH: Oh yes, shortly after I ended up going on a trip to Austria. It was beautiful but cold. I am certainly powered by the sun. After traveling through Europe, I worked in a country coaching inn and then landed in the Roundhouse Recording Studio, where I had to manage the office and the appointments.

OBSERVER: This was in the 70s?

TITCH: Yes, so there was a very popular English rock band called Uriah Heep, who would record at the studio. KISS was a support band for Uriah Heep, but then it went from opening for Uriah to taking Heep on the road as the supporting act. We had nothing digital in those days, instead, I had this big booking book with all the acts noted down. So, I was paging through the bookings book and I could see Queen booked in at 2 pm, every day for like 3 months. So, I asked the tape operator–"Why does the Queen need so much time to record her Christmas Day speech?" He roared with laughter at my ignorance that I had never heard of the group Queen. One particular afternoon, around 4 o'clock, the heavy door of the studio pulled open, and a long-haired man went straight through towards the recording room, I said, "Excuse me! Excuse me!" as I sprang out of my chair and rushed to block his entry into the recording room. I didn't want to lose my job by letting some unknown man into a room with expensive equipment and master tapes.

"Can I help you?" I asked. He shot me a glare, looked at me up and down, and said, "Do you know who I am?" I said, "I haven't got a clue. If you tell me who you are, I'll tell you who I am and then maybe I'll let you go." He turned and walked out. About an hour later, Brian May, who I had met before, came and asked "Have you seen Freddy?" I said, "Uh…, Does Freddy have kind of long hair and buck teeth? And a hairy chest?" Brian said, "Yeah, yeah. Has he gone to the loo?"

When I told him what had unfolded, he just said "F*****g Queen!" It was hilarious. Later, we held the launch party in the studio for Bohemian Rhapsody, as it had just been released as a single. There were several others, like Ozzy Osbourne, Osibisa, Mike Oldfield, Motörhead, and Coliseum.

OBSERVER: How did you manage to get yourself into these serendipitous situations?

TITCH: I don't know if it was serendipitous. A lot of the things I've done in my life have been for survival. When I first landed in the UK, I started working in a country coaching inn. It was there I had met Bobbi who was the nanny for Jerry and Lillian Bron. They owned the Bron Organization, which was a major music company. They needed an urgent replacement at one of their studios, and Bobbi recommended me. I have never been shy to learn from or mingle with people and that has certainly taken me places. I was living in South Kensington at some point and rented a beautiful apartment. Turns out it was owned by Camilla (who's now married to Prince Charles) and her sister. At that time, she was still married to her first husband. My friend and I were painting up the cupboards after getting her sister's permission when we found Camilla's invitations to the palace as a debutante and love letters written to her.

Not everything has been rosy and fun all the time. I remember when I had to close my event management business during the recession of the 90s. It was a terrible recession and a lot of my friends had lost their jobs; they had lost their houses because the mortgage couldn't be paid and many divorces had happened. However, things do turn around even after life takes a dive. I got offered a job in the Middle East and that was my next adventure.

OBSERVER: Is carefree the same as careless?

TITCH: Not at all. I have enjoyed my life thoroughly, but never at the cost of slacking off and being lazy. I guess it was family values that were instilled in us when we were children. Never, ever, in my life have I called in sick even when I was invited to Paris for lunch on a private jet. Trust is important, you should never misplace that. I have always believed that sickness would actually strike me down if I lied about it. You must learn how to take care and clean up after yourself by taking responsibility for your actions. I never asked my parents for money once after I left home. Even though we had a maid, our parents taught my sister and me to clean the dishes and our clothes. When you do not do that, you become an outgrown baby masquerading as an adult.

In South Africa, growing up, there were a lot of superstitions and myths. People believed in witch doctors who would go about casting spells and wishing ill on people. Our maid, Dorothy, believed the washing machine was the white man's way of spreading cancer. One Sunday, my father, who was a Senior Manager at a mine, went to the site because of a very serious rock fall underground. They had to get all the guys out from underground. There was a guy that came out and his body was smashed. The doctor came to visit him frequently. Hard to believe how this guy survived. Another guy landed up with a scratch on his arm, but he believed the witch doctor put a spell on him and he died within a day. It's the mind. I have seen so much of it in my career so far. So much of it. And you see mind control in the states, in the military as well. So be careful of what you think, but do not stop yourself from living and enjoying your life.

OBSERVER: How are you so active and healthy at 71?

TITCH: My plastic surgeon friend, Dr Raed, is always suggesting that he can help me anti-age, and I say oh, no, no, no, no. I have earned these wrinkles on my face. They are my character; they have a story to tell. And there are not that many. They are part of my history. I smoked cigarettes and cigars often and drank, but I had to leave all of that behind. When the C5 vertebrae in my neck began degenerating, the allopathic doctors wanted to hack into me with a knife. It was after I said no that my friend Jyoti introduced me to Siddhi Samadhi Yoga (SSY), which completely changed my life. I became a pure vegetarian. I did breathing exercises every day. I meditated every day, and it changed the way I saw my world. It's funny because I was so skeptical and was expecting some mumbo jumbo out of this guru's mouth when I saw him.

OBSERVER: What was the first thing he said to you when you met him?

TITCH: All disease is what we put across our lips, what we eat. It becomes our body. The second thing was we do not breathe deeply enough. We do not get enough oxygen. When I first met him and he greeted me, I snapped at him and said "I've got a headache." as if it was his fault. He just sweetly smiled at me, took my hand, and he just pressed on the side of each finger. By the time he got to the tenth finger, the headache was gone. Along with the pain, my skepticism was also gone. So, it takes an experience to really understand what is possible for you. Skepticism will forever keep you outside the fence, in the cold. My friend used to joke that before yoga, I was a rottweiler with lipstick. After yoga, I became much more tranquil and more detached.

OBSERVER: You became calmer and more detached, but still your adventures continued, just that they've been filled with a lot of compassion and care. You started the ARRAY Foundation, which is meant to give light and a new life to many people suffering from spinal injuries by making them independent and employable. How did that start and what is your vision for it?

TITCH: One of my batch mates in SSY once spoke on the radio about being a volunteer in Dubai, in hospitals, visiting patients in the hospital, and prisoners in jail. I called him up and said I wanted to do it to give back what I could. I went to the Rashid Hospital, walked around with these people, going to all these different beds, saying hello to all these poor souls that were there. Once there was a young East European sailor, whose legs had been deeply marred by thick steel ropes. It was terrible, and he was very depressed. I was chatting with him. The ship had already left port, so he was alone in a strange country, in a strange hospital. Nobody to talk to. So I said to him, "I'll come back and visit you on Tuesday." And he was so grateful. I took him a book to read.

There was also a guy named Nazirullah from Afghanistan, who was working illegally in Dubai because many of these guys come and work illegally on the building sites. Unfortunately, he had his right arm amputated in a cement mixer, and he was in tears. He wanted to write a letter to his mom, but his right hand had been chopped off. I rushed to the stationery shop near the hospital and picked up some pencils, a notebook, and a children's book on how to write the letters A, B, and C. I gave it to him and said "Now you're going to learn to write with your left hand, and at the same time you're going to learn the English alphabet." There was an American Professor admitted next to Nazirullah. I turned to him and said, "You're sitting in the bed next to him, and you're a professor, and you can help him, okay?" On Sunday night, when I returned, the entire book was filled. I turned to the professor, who said, "This guy... I don't think he slept. He's hungry for it." He did it all with his left hand! I made him write the letter, and I posted it to his mother. When he was being deported, I got him sweets and some money, but they are not supposed to be given anything. The police said no at first but then obliged and asked me "Are you a Muslim? Why are you helping him this much?" I said "Why? Should I be a Muslim to help? I'm a volunteer at Rashid Hospital. I go there and see what I can do for people."

There are many people in a state of hopelessness and despair because their lives have turned upside down because of unforeseeable injuries. Even fully able-bodied people feel stuck in their lives. Can you imagine the plight of these people? I know how competent and motivated people who have lost mobility can be if we give them the right guidance, treatment, and training. That's why I have been spending years of my life and my savings trying to make the ARRAY Foundation Rehabilitation Centre a reality. Throughout the process, people have cheated me, turned me down, and ignored me, but the vision still lives on. If it's meant to be, we will find the land and gather the funds needed to support this self-sustaining project that can bring a new start to so many lives.

OBSERVER: We often underestimate the power of desire; it can move mountains if it wants to.

TITCH: I think it's the innate drive for exploration and just doing something with no regrets. I always believe that there is more to see, do, and experience than I already have, and each new venture brings something interesting to it. Plus, now I can never run out of stories to tell! I have seen bizarre things in life and been in even more bizarre scenarios, but it just makes me believe that a lot of amazing things are possible.

So why not be the thing that makes those circumstances possible for yourself and others?

*You must learn to think for yourself and take ownership of that. If you do not control your mind, someone else will, and that takes all your power away from you. You already have everything you need; air in your lungs, a passionate heart, and a peaceful mind are all you will ever need. It's not travel, but strong intentions and choices that take you places.*

## Philomathy: The power of being hungry for knowledge and the right networking

*Dr. Arasu is an Associate Professor of Virology at the University of Maryland, School of Dentistry, who has been loved and appreciated by his students for his way of teaching and the confidence he instills in them. Despite having challenges learning at school and financial constraints, his passion for knowledge and his will to succeed never faded.*

OBSERVER: Can you share some of the most challenging instances in your life?

ARASU: I was born to middle-class parents living in a village. Both of my parents were elementary school educated till fourth or fifth grade, I suppose. They knew how to read and write, that is it. A lot of their personal aspirations remained unfulfilled. So, they motivated me to study, which I am grateful for. However, they could not give me any guidance on what I should study and why. In those days, there was very little awareness of children's learning abilities. You were smart or foolish. It was recently, after several decades of living and learning, that I realized I have ADHD and dyslexia. Had I known that before, it would have helped me understand why I learn differently than others. I was an above-average student. These two challenges kept me from discovering my potential as a learner and prevented me from shining in my early academic years.

OBSERVER: When did you realize you had ADHD and dyslexia?

ARASU: It was diagnosed 10 years back. I was watching a program on ADHD. I told my daughter, "Hey, it looks like it's me." Then I went and got diagnosed. However, there are great examples of people succeeding in life and doing a great job despite learning disabilities. Instead of seeing it as a hurdle, it's more of an off-beaten path to learning, as the brain processes information differently. Woodrow Wilson is one of my favorite examples of how a person with ADHD and strong dyslexia can perform his job and excel at it. As a strong dyslexic and the President of the United States, he could not read until he was 10 years old. Wilson's father taught him the art of debating to support his learning and overcome writing challenges. Wilson became a lawyer and a US president who received the

Nobel Peace Prize in recognition of his Fourteen Points peace program and the establishment of the League of Nations. Kids and parents need to know that personalizing learning to suit the student's needs can lead to them doing wonders. I did not have that opportunity, and I also did not select academic topics to study, considering my strengths.

OBSERVER: How do you think people pick their careers and why did you choose to be a professor?

ARASU: In Asian societies, there is pressure to either become a doctor or an engineer. Everything else is subpar. Now, things are changing, but there is still a need for a lot more awareness. Mathematics was not my favorite subject, so I opted for biology and applied for an undergraduate degree in medicine. However, I struggled to make it through there and shine. Looking back, I think I should have taken up language, psychology, history, or sociology, but could not because art and humanities did not rank high in people's perception of success. Not selecting the right career path despite being eager to learn and grow in life is a struggle for many people and a concoction of dissatisfaction. Had I taken up a subject that I am naturally inclined towards, I would have shined much better by enjoying it and not feeling like it was excessive work. Financial considerations compelled us to pursue a field that prioritizes high pay over personal interest.

Picking a career without proper guidance is like shooting darts in the dark and hoping to hit the target. From my experience as a professor for 30 years, I have seen thousands of students and come to the same conclusion. Which is to choose your studies based on your personality type and your core interests. As each personality is innately capable of handling certain tasks and concepts better than others, awareness of your strengths and weaknesses is important to be confident and succeed at whatever you are doing. OBSERVER: Whichever subject you pick, if you persist at it long enough with dedication, you can see results. Do you agree with that notion?

ARASU: Yes, that is right. I agree. If you persist enough, you can do it. Despite the setbacks I faced, I could succeed based on good contacts and network. I respect people, enjoy listening to different perspectives, and am naturally curious.

I sought the insights of my friends to make a major decision, like choosing the right college or job where I would be placed well. Each friend of mine contributed in their own way. My friends helped me make eight out of the 10 or 12 major life decisions. "Hey, here is a job. Here is an opening. You can apply." That is a tremendous feeling, to have that support and concern. This differs from force or peer pressure. It's simply possibilities and opportunities. In the end, it's for us to decide. That is one thing. The second thing is persistence. I do not give up. I don't get frustrated about the how, when, etc. There is a tendency to not lose hope.

OBSERVER: That is a key quality that can be innate for some and requires practice by others, I suppose. How did the lack of frustration help you on your journey?

ARASU: I completed my MSc and my MPhil with consistent efforts, and I immediately got a teaching position at St. Joseph College, and next year I got a permanent Assistant Professor position. There was a 24-day workshop for college teachers at an all-India level. There were 24 panelists, which included Indian scientists who were trained in Australia, Canada, France, and Germany, coming back here to train more teachers. They were placed at premier Indian Research institutions like the Tata Institute of Fundamental Research and the Indian Institute of Science. The atmosphere created by them during the workshop was phenomenal. One of my friends alerted me to this opportunity and suggested I attend. If I had not attended, I would not have met the trainers and scientists, and would not have been selected for a professorial position in America. Life would have been very different. Frustration blocks the mind from grasping onto opportunities, keeping you stuck where you are, and leaving little room for exploration.

OBSERVER: Opportunities come through exploration and just showing up seems to hold tremendous power in orchestrating fruitful events. What's the next step after showing up?

ARASU: The next step would certainly be networking.

OBSERVER: You have built a very nice and supportive network, which many people struggle with. What do you think worked in your favor while building such a supportive network?

ARASU: I think it's just being a very genuine person. I have attracted meaningful relationships by adding insight and value to others and being open to receiving that from others. Even if it's a few minutes, one year, or two years of a person's life. I always had a deep intention that I want to help them, and that they want to help me. I can share what I have, and when we all do it with the spirit of uplifting one another, we all will go to different places. Cutting out prolonged small talk, speaking with genuine care, concern, and information. So, I learn more useful information and perspectives, so that I can be of value to myself and others, and engage in noteworthy conversations. That value will come back to me. No nonsense. No shallow conversations. I don't like it, as it's not a good use of my time or energy.

OBSERVER: Finding friends and peers with a collaborative growth mindset is nothing but an asset.

ARASU: You must be the person who does not see everyone else as your competitors. That is important to find more meaningful collaborators in your life. It does not matter what background you come from. It matters who you present yourself as.

OBSERVER: Would you always take the initiative to go and talk to people?

ARASU: Reasonably well. I don't see too many people who do that better than me. Whomever I interact with in more than a formal conversation, I wish them well. I care for them. And if they say something, I am supportive of them. It's mutual. As a result, I made strong connections that have helped me throughout my life. When I first moved to America, it was tough getting used to the new way of living, cost of expenditure, etc. My American friends helped me a lot so did my Indian friends and Tamil community. Even though there were few opportunities in my field at the time, because I had made a lasting impression on people, they remembered me and offered me work. I did not chase work. If he hasn't asked me, somebody else will —was the empowering belief I had running, now that I think about it.

OBSERVER: Along with caring, you mentioned you were naturally curious, so does that translate into asking insightful questions?

ARASU: Yes, good point. There is always something to learn from one another. So, the more meaningful questions you ask, the more meaningful conversations you will have. Rather than assuming, ask. Do not leave stuff up in the air.

OBSERVER: To balance one's personal interests and those of others, an individual must stay grounded. One of the best ways to be a grounded person is to have strong roots. Is that true for you?

ARASU: Definitely. Roots were strong. I had this sense of responsibility for helping others and taking care of myself, no matter what. My parents gave me a lot of values and direction in that aspect. I think a lot of young kids these days wish to have this guidance and supportive peers because there is a lot of peer pressure to do all kinds of nonsense, but there is not enough peer pressure to grow strongly and admirably.

*Happiness, confidence, patience, productivity, and synergy are important words to keep in mind as you try to navigate life. You do not learn these qualities; you experience them. They are innate, obscured by the fortress of our doubts and fears. Start poking holes in those walls with your eagerness to learn, curiosity, and compassion so that you tap into all that which has always been yours to enjoy.*

## Wonder Woman: The power and the vision of the feminine

*What doesn't kill you makes you stronger —*
*Friedrich Nietzsche*
*As a man thinketh, so is he–Bible Proverbs 23:7*

OBSERVER: Could you tell us a little about who you are and where you come from?

WINFRIDA: Hello, my name is Winfrida Elipokea Kanuya. I am from Tanzania and I am very proud to be a Tanzanian. You will find it on the east coast of Africa. Growing up as a black African young lady in our society has not been an easy ride. There are a lot of expectations which the society places on you. I am the firstborn in my family, but my mom's only child. So, I have step-siblings, but my mom, as a single mom, went through innumerable challenges to create a stable and loving home for me. And, I'm so grateful for that, because that love, values, and nurture have become a part of my nature. I did not see the fact that my mom was a single mother as a weakness. I took it as a sign of strength instead.

OBSERVER: We know that both men and women are important, but what makes you adore women?

WINFRIDA: Life has shown me that sometimes if the only choice a woman has is to take care of her family, despite all odds, she will live for that choice. You never know what is possible until you see it. So, watching my mom set a great example of a strong woman who can gracefully do so much on her own, made me believe that I too have that power in me. In a patriarchal society, where a woman is not considered an equal, a woman can go on to do great things. That doesn't mean that men can't. Men can, and society has publicly celebrated their achievements for decades. However, women's achievements are often undermined and swiped under the rug as a duty.

Being raised by a single mother, I am in awe and appreciate more deeply the wonders that women can do. Women can be seen as weak, vulnerable, and emotional, but women can take care of their families even if they do not have the support of a man. A woman's life carries on and evolves to be whole and complete for herself and her kids, even in the absence of a man. This experience has created a strong drive in me to have a clear vision for myself as a confident, self-sufficient, independent woman. I need to study well. I need to have my personal source of income before and after marriage. Looking for these things in a man whom I will either get married to or whom maybe I'll be in a relationship with will just create co-dependency and make me feel like I am not enough on my own. The value of freedom that comes from self-dependency and a self-assured personality has set the foundation in my life, which I can never explain enough. This clear vision, independence, and strength save you when you are in an environment that is not the most supportive.

OBSERVER: Do you think our environment shapes us?

WINFRIDA: I didn't grow up in a rich family or a rich society, I just grew up in a middle-income family. In the neighborhood where I lived, you really had to search for opportunities. I think that helped me develop a sharp mind that is always on the lookout for seeing the best in everything. I learn through observing, and I learn through others. I've always been this way since I was young, even though I don't know why. Whoever it was, neighbors or anybody else, I never judged them. I was always open to learning from others' words and actions. These observations motivated me and showed me what I can aspire to be and it helped me stay on track in my life. Also, they say that if you can learn through others, others will learn through you. Everyone is unique and if their path intertwines with yours, there is something in their journey which can enrich yours if you observe it closely enough. We can learn what not to do as well, even that is important to understand the consequences of poor choices. Everyone has their own experience in life. That means if you talk to at least ten people, you'll have ten unique experiences and perspectives. That broadens your mental horizons and elevates your perception of the world and yourself.

OBSERVER: That is an interesting perspective. Do you believe that our perception of the world determines our experience of it?

WINFRIDA: Yes, I do. Along with a healthy perception, if you are a person who takes action, your life will change for the better. You would think we would have a lot of financial problems, but we didn't. We were not rich, but did not see life as a day-to-day struggle. We were happy with whatever we were blessed with. Having your basic needs met, such as education, is something I am grateful for. My mom didn't want me to lack access to basic needs, and she didn't want me to lack education. She was always making sure that I got everything I truly needed to grow into a well-balanced and mature adult. I'm so proud of my mom because she's a fighter. In life, we are exposed to different situations, and by experiencing those situations, they can either teach us and change us for the better, or they can destroy us and completely ruin our lives.

Perspective or mindset is so important because how someone chooses to see the situation is how it will turn out to be. That is because how we choose to see the problem is exactly how we will choose to find the best solution for that problem. If you are unable to handle the problems popping up in your life and lose hope, it's easy to slip into depression, stress, and all the other mental health issues. However, if you see it as —this is a problem and one day I will be able to tackle it, then you will ask yourself, "How can I do it? Let me reach out to some people who have gone through this problem." You do not wait for the support; you actively seek it.

OBSERVER: How has education helped your perspective?

WINFRIDA: I love studying. My favorite subject was and still is, mathematics. I love mathematics because it challenges me and helps me see a problem for what it is. It just needs to be solved and there is always some solution to a problem. How you choose to tackle it will determine how it's going to bring you the result. It can happen as soon as possible or it can be delayed because of how you choose to solve the problem.

I have a diploma in water supply and sanitation engineering. I just love water. Studying water supply and sanitation, I think, was one of the best things I could ever do. I am very happy I made that decision because it taught me so much that I did not know. I had no clue what it was at first, but when I studied about it, I understood how we take the simplest things for granted. You know, water has no other replacement in this world. You can never replace water. Water is water. It moves, it adapts to the vessel it is in. That lesson I learned personally as well because my life as a university student was not that easy. One encounters multiple challenges while interacting with different people from different societies, and dealing with roommates. I had to adapt. I am a very adaptive person because of my faith in God. God has played a very big part in my life and is still playing a part in helping me with my challenges.

OBSERVER: Can you share why your faith in God has been your pillar of support?

WINFRIDA: I am incredibly grateful, just so grateful to God for everything. Being in the state of gratitude keeps me from taking things for granted, and seeing the beauty even on dark days. God gave me wonderful friends. My friends and I still love each other, and we still communicate. We hold each other's hand through the challenges we go through. It's not always easy to meet the right people, but with a pure heart and faith in God, it has been possible. Even though you have your friends, you can't always tell them everything. But just one hug from those people. You have that "Yeah, this feels like home" moment. You may encounter jealous people as well. They just talk to you, laugh at you, laugh with you, and they want to know your weakness, your weakest point so that they can strike you. I think I came to know that quite late, but no harm has come upon me, so I am grateful.

Throughout my life, I think God has been always there for me because whenever there is a challenge, I call God and He answers. It may not be immediate, but He answers. If I have to sum up my life in one sentence, I will just say, it is by God and it is through God that I've come this far. When I started working at the Mbulu Water Supply and Sanitation Authority as a volunteer, I encountered different challenges in adapting to the new environment. As a newbie, you feel overwhelmed, and when you do things, you think that everything you're doing is wrong. It's hard, but you learn to persist when you have faith. I adapted to the environment in just about two months.

OBSERVER: What has been your key takeaway from your life so far?

WINFRIDA: Being a black woman in this society is a bit challenging. That's good, however, because the more the challenges I experienced, the stronger I became. It has made me evolve not only physically but also mentally, influencing how I see things and how I solve life's problems, you know? I live in faith and act with courage. The challenges I've faced have given me the ability to see life from different perspectives. I think that's the best gift that life can give you.

OBSERVER: Thank you, Winfrida.

*I don't want to be remembered for the work I did, the many organizations I worked for, many positions I held at the office or in my country.*

*I don't want to be remembered for the criticism I made, the abusive language I spoke or the negative attitude I showed.*

*I don't want to be remembered by a great name, amazing business, good ideas, or material possessions.*

*I don't want to be remembered by the name of my mother, my father, my rich relative, my sister or brother, by nicknames, middle name, or surname.*

*But, I want to be remembered. Yes, I want to be remembered by the living character, the love I shared with all people big and small, rich and poor, spiritual and pagans, family, and strangers.*

*Because I don't want to be remembered as the child of the world but rather as a child of God.*
*—  Winfrida Elipokea Kanuya*

*We use a lot of labels to identify ourselves, but none of it means more than who you really felt you were and what you made others feel around you. Faith is the thread of unconditional love that holds us up when everything seems to be crashing down. Faith in yourself and consequently in a supreme universal power called God is what turns obstacles into miracles. Living a life of passion and devotion is one of the most fulfilling things you can do. It takes courage, though. Find it, because it is worth it.*

# THE WHY

# CHAPTER 4

# The Adversity Advantage?

People love a good struggle. The drama, trauma, intrigue, lows, highs, and uncertainty of struggle hook the human mind and heart. Look at any movie, advertisement, or fiction book; the story will have a low and a high, as it's a hero's journey. Without it, you don't feel like you went on a ride. Life, too, is just a ride that is meant to shape the traveler's perspective and personality. The ride is why you're here, so you might as well learn to enjoy it. The struggle is simply a lesson, and every setback is just a slight redirection asking you to recalibrate your response to life. Every human being has to meet struggle at some point in their lives, although the types, intensity, and duration of struggle will vary from person to person. Growth doesn't mean growing up age-wise or just accumulating assets. Growth happens when there is an internal change in one's perspective, nervous and biochemical response, and actions. The struggle is the catalyst needed to go on this journey of growth and experience the beauty and power of triumphing over all your challenges. You need your lowest points and the consequent dissatisfaction to realize you need to have more courage to go against your negative spiral and create. Discomfort and dissatisfaction are the precursors of problem-solving, as constraints foster creativity.

Notice how we attach a lot of respect to overcoming a struggle, because, of course, it's not an easy task to persist through life's daunting challenges one after the other. Acknowledging that is very important. However, this glorification of the struggle, and yearning for the respect earned from the struggle, further perpetuates the saga of unending trials and tribulations.

All the setbacks, the pain, the disappointment, the failure, the rejection —all of it happens with the intention of removing from our system everything we are not. I am not the anxiety that comes from declining finances. I am not the pain that comes from being rejected by someone I love. I am not the self-doubt and pity that comes from failing to achieve my dreams. I am not what the world wants me to be. I am who I am. I am whole and I am complete because of my innate ability to transcend and grow out of these circumstances and be who I want to be. If there is something undesirable that keeps showing up, what small shift can you bring in your thoughts, feelings, or actions that will turn even the undesirable event into a happy happenstance? It begins with seeding the belief "Everything is always working out *for* me and happening *for* me, not *to* me. If I get what I want now, I won. If I didn't get what I wanted I got a valuable lesson instead, which if applied correctly is just going to make me win bigger!" Resilient reintegration happens when a person responds to disruption in a way that leads to a personal breakthrough or insight. The challenge itself brings about the discovery or enhancement of resilient characteristics within an individual. Individuals possess genetic potential beyond their awareness, and disruptions serve to reveal this potential.[10]

As children, life is a playground, where infinite possibilities exist and there's joy in everything, but as we grow into adults, that very life becomes a battleground to fight the limitations placed on us and chase our shadows. It's time we drop the fight within ourselves and return to the playground to come up with better games to play as adults, ones that are not built upon fear, loss, and struggle but are centered around courage, compassion, and clarity. Every day, you are born again. You can choose to be born again by letting the old self go.

Emotional addiction manifests in the lives of the addict in a series of typical behaviors, such as constant venting, the need to relive negative experiences, and unconsciously seeking relationships and situations that activate their hit emotions by triggering feelings of uncertainty and abandonment.

Let's talk about the adversity advantage—there's no doubt that adversity helps in preparing and training for harder times. Think of it like muscle-building. When you lift weights, you're tearing tiny fibers in your muscles, and it's the body's repair process that makes them stronger. Adversity works similarly for the mind. It increases your risk-taking capacity and makes you mentally and emotionally stronger. You learn to anticipate risks, and you're not afraid to deal with them. The stress that adversity brings pushes you to evolve and adapt, just as those torn muscle fibers heal stronger.

However, just like the pain from overdoing your workout, too much adversity without recovery leads to burnout, injury, and exhaustion. Ever seen meerkats? Meerkats are a type of mongoose that stand upright, constantly on alert for predators. Overexposure to adversity essentially locks your brain into survival mode. In this state, your nervous system is wired to fend off threats. This leaves little room for creation, imagination, or rational thinking because the brain is primarily focused on survival.

You won't even realize when life turned you into a meerkat who's always looking to defend. The sympathetic nervous system, which controls your fight-or-flight response, is in overdrive, releasing stress hormones like cortisol. Although these hormones are helpful in short bursts, when elevated for long periods, they wear down the body and mind. When you're in this constant state of fight-or-flight, your energy is consumed by vigilance—guarding yourself and fending off perceived threats. It's almost like trying to paint a masterpiece while standing guard at a fortress. You're always waiting for the next attack, so there's no room for creative flow or vision.

Civilization, human progress, and innovation weren't born out of survival alone. The most advanced societies arose when humans shifted from simply surviving to thriving. They had to take their minds off mere survival to build art, philosophy, technology, and new ways of thinking. In biological terms, this represents a shift from the primitive functions of the reptilian brain elements (which govern survival instincts) to the more evolved neocortex, where creativity, abstract thought, and vision emerge.[11,12] Consider the example of early humans. Yes, survival against predators and harsh environments was necessary, but it was when they could sit around the fire, safe and nurtured, that they began storytelling, crafting tools, and envisioning futures that extended beyond mere survival. These moments of security allowed their brains to tap into the expansive imaginative capacities of the neocortex.

It's not just adversity that defines our lives today. It's about the delicate equilibrium between adversity and nurturing. Just as plants need sunlight but also water and soil nutrients, humans need challenges to grow, but they also need rest, support, and the space to create. Too much of either leads to stagnation—either overprotected and under-stimulated or overexerted and burned out.

To have balance every day of your life is a tough feat because unexpected things pop up from time to time. The kind of balance you want will differ from person to person. Some people need it daily, some weekly, and some monthly. Go with what fits you, not what fits others. Facing adversity forces you to grow, but nurturing environments allow you to become visionary, creative, and capable of using your full range of talents. Moments of peaceful silence, connection, and creativity are the less-trodden but more fulfilling ways to meet a more amusing version of you that has gone beyond survival mode and created an inner sanctuary for yourself.

Despite facing the same type of pain, some are able to move on much more quickly than others with the involuntary coping mechanism of forgetfulness. They tend to forget things easily, including many bad memories. In a way, their memory issues seem to have a silver lining. Unless they consciously try to recall that a particular situation was painful or tough, their mind and body naturally let go of most of those emotions. Because they don't remember them, they can quickly focus on the next important task, free from the clutter of painful thoughts and feelings. I used to hate the fact that I was forgetful, but it was the best way I could handle life at the time.

This sentiment was echoed by my chartered account friend as well. Then she mentioned another insight that clicked something in my brain. "Maybe another reason I don't dwell on the past is that I live in the moment so deeply that I don't feel the need to go back to it. For example, if someone or something hurts me, I cry it out. I let myself fully experience the pain, feeling every emotion deeply and intensely in that moment. Once I've felt all the pain I could from that experience, it's as if my mind says–I'm done with this now, and it's time to move on. Since I've already processed the emotions, there's no need to revisit them, and I can move forward"–she said.

This is such a powerful thing as I realized how we take our tears for granted, seeing them as weak. Inadvertent tears are not a product of the logical conscious mind, rather they are the expression of the emotional subconscious mind that is on autopilot. When you cry, you are emptying a part of yourself and creating more space for new things to enter your mind and body. The self-talk that you have right as you finish crying is very important as it's readily accepted by your subconscious mind in that heightened state of emotion. Be very careful of the meaning you attach to your tears and the experience producing them as they become your vantage point for the next batch of moments in your reality.

Everybody is born a bundle of joy, love, and happiness—pure and untainted. There are no filters, no impressions, nothing imprinted yet. But as we grow up, conditioning begins, and filters form. We start facing challenges, and often, we're not equipped or guided on how to handle them. This lack of guidance leads us to question,

"Why is this happening to me?" You end up feeling lost like you're stuck in a dark place, and it can feel like the world is against you.

But that's not true. It's not the fact that we have challenges; it's the fact that we don't know how to shine a light on them. That's why we feel like we're in the dark, completely lost. The unknown seems terrifying and shrouded in darkness because we don't understand it. Life is a journey of moving through that darkness, expanding your perspective, and learning to interpret the challenges you face—understanding who you really are, what you're meant to do, and how you're supposed to be. Relearning all of that is the real knowledge you need to acquire in this lifetime.

How you see things—your challenges, yourself, and the world around you—comes from turning on the light within yourself. Just like a solitary lighthouse shining light onto the darkness unbothered by the rising tides of water crashing against it. Not only are you guiding yourself but you also become a beacon for other people to learn from. This light is your own— created by the strength, trust, and clarity within you. Your circumstances do not define you and neither does your past. The only thing that defines you is your ability to observe and mold a future out of your observation. Our doubts and fears will always try to keep us in darkness.

As long as you stay in the dark and avoid asking the right questions, you'll never find the answers you need. But when you set the intention to observe, you start throwing light on your challenges, and understanding follows. Question, seek guidance, and start interpreting why things happen the way they do, and you'll realize that you were never really lost. You just couldn't see through your doubts and fears. To find the light and see what you already possess, you need to let go of the blinders that have been placed on you. These blinders make you feel like the world is a dark place, but in reality, it's not. Letting go of these filters means dissolving your ego, dissolving the idea that "I know everything." or "This is the only way there is." or "I am not good enough." or "Nothing changes."

"I know everything" —You can never learn anything else that can help you grow in a rapidly changing world.

"This is the only way there is" —You have hit a perpetual dead end on a lonely road.

"I am not good enough" —You will automatically lose interest in trying again.

"Nothing changes" —You have condemned yourself to a life of stagnation.

Every word you use holds some meaning to your inner self even when no one else is listening. Your words are buttons pushing your psychological states and vice versa. So choose the words that carry a psychological benefit. In general, avoid the extremes of always and never. Life does not thrive at the poles, rather it blooms in the field between them.

Our struggles shape us, yes, but don't let them own you by being defined by them. Being fixated on your troubles and overly proud of your struggles means living a life where nothing comes easy. Accept your struggles, thank them, and set yourself free from constantly having to prove your worth. Choose to be defined not by the things you hate but by the things you love and the world will see your worth without you even trying to prove it.

Every challenge you face is simply trying to get your attention. It's saying, "Look at me! Pay attention!" so that you can grow stronger and more capable of handling it. Once you do, the challenge often rewards you with something greater. It's like life's way of testing you, to see if you're ready for the next level. And it's up to you to either say, "Challenge accepted" or to run from it. But even if you run, that challenge will come back and chase you down. So, you might as well accept it and make it legendary.

**Actionable point:** Observe what you are allowing and what you are not. Are you allowing yourself to go through experiences that you have consciously or unconsciously chosen? Or are you desperately trying to force/control them, which is only prolonging the struggle? Are you allowing yourself to still love yourself through all the inadequacy and the pain? That is how you realize you are enough for yourself, even when life's circumstances scream otherwise.

Make a list of all the things you are trying to control and set the intention to drop the fight. Next to each of them write a reason —why to drop the fight, starting with the words "I allow myself to..." That can be "I allow myself to be happy", "I allow myself to receive love/support/money", "I allow myself to rest", "I allow myself to be self-assured", "I allow myself to be brave" and so on.

# CHAPTER 5

# Factors of Resilience

Some people may naturally have a greater inclination to be resilient and perform best under pressure, but it's definitely a skill that can be learned and an extremely important one at that. Resilience is built over time as you start to prioritize your ambition, your desire, your intentions, and the things you love over the things that you are afraid of. Fear only goes as deep as you allow it to. Confront it and it will leave, run from it and it will thrive and claim more of your space.

Resilience in both animals and humans is influenced by various factors including biological, psychological, social, and environmental elements. These specific factors differ between species and between individuals of the same species, but there are also many similarities.

## Biological Factors

*Genetic Predisposition*

Genetic factors may play a role in determining an individual's baseline resilience. Some individuals may be inherently more resilient because of genes that affect traits such as temperament, stress response, and neuroplasticity. For example, a study found that certain genetic variations related to the regulation of serotonin (one of the feel-good hormones) were associated with higher levels of resilience in individuals facing chronic stress.[13] However, we still lack concrete evidence pinpointing which genes govern emotional resilience. Don't let genes become your excuse. YOU control how you feel. How you feel impacts how much you can heal and carry on in life. Genes are NOT the end-all-be-all. They can and do change, depending upon you and your internal/external milieu. Even if there is a pattern of fearfulness in your family, it's up to you to decide if you want to continue that pattern or break out of it.

## *Brain Plasticity*

One of the most potent ways to break out of an unhealthy pattern is to replace it with a healthier pattern. The brain is astonishingly good at this, as it can reorganize itself and form new neural connections (neuroplasticity) that are crucial for resilience. Both animals and humans can adapt to challenges by rewiring neural circuits, enabling them to cope with stress and recover from adversity. Neuroimaging studies show that individuals who engage in mindfulness meditation exhibit structural changes in brain regions associated with emotion regulation and stress resilience, such as the prefrontal cortex, default mode network (DMN), and amygdala.[14,15] DMN is a system of interconnections in your brain that becomes active when you are lost in your thoughts and disconnected from the external environment.[16,17]

Ever been on autopilot? A mode where you are doing your routine tasks, but your attention is elsewhere, busy daydreaming and introspecting. The activity of this DMN can invoke creativity in you or cause you to mull over your worries depending upon your attitude and tendencies in life, which have wired in some neuronal patterns in your brain. For example, DMN is more active in the brains of lonely people who spend a lot of time thinking about the past and the future while feeling worried and anxious.[17–20] When you do things outside your comfort zone, your brain needs to learn and process information faster and cannot stay in autopilot mode anymore, pushing you to think and grow in the present moment. This is why the magic of growth and success lies outside your comfort zone, where you take charge and start piloting your life consciously.

Imagine your brain as a busy airport. The DMN is like the air traffic control tower, constantly managing flights—these flights represent your thoughts. Some planes (thoughts) have been taking off and landing in the same pattern for years, creating well-worn paths in your mind. The DMN's job is to keep these planes moving smoothly, but over time, this means the same thoughts and behaviors are repeated, even when you're trying to introduce alternative routes. When we're lost in thought, replaying memories, or worrying about the future, the DMN is fully active. It's like the air traffic controller endlessly rerouting planes along the same paths, even when we want to break out of the cycle. The key to turning down this constant mental chatter isn't by trying to shut down the airport or micromanage each flight. Step out of that control tower and start gathering real-time observations of the new route you want to explore.

It's not enough to intellectually understand the change you want—you need to fully immerse yourself in the experience of it. By deeply engaging with what's happening now, you allow your mind to adjust naturally to fresh paths. The more you practice being present, the more comfortable and familiar this new route becomes, and soon, your brain will begin to shift its focus from the old to the new without you having to force it.

*Physical Health*

Animals and humans with robust physical health may be better equipped to withstand stressors and recover from setbacks. This is because stress is of two types–Eustress and Distress. Not all stress is bad stress aka distress. Eustress is the good or positive stress that lasts for a short time, energizing you and motivating you to make a change. It gives us a positive outlook and makes us capable of overcoming obstacles and sickness. If we had no stress at all, we would not have the motivation to move and grow, making the mind and the body inactive and dull. Whereas too much stress then manifests as pain, anger, and anxiety. Exercise is a great example of eustress, as exercise, although strenuous, promotes neuroplasticity and the growth of cells and blood vessels in the brain.[21]

So exercise is not just for losing weight or building muscle on the exterior; internally, it improves our ability to think through difficult situations, practice self-discipline, and make the best decisions for ourselves. During covid-19 lockdown, people who increased their exercise levels as a coping mechanism significantly built their resilience and could moderate the impact of the pandemic on their lives.[22] Your mind and body are partners in peace and crime. If your mental health is taking a deep dive, start focusing on your physical health, which will automatically nudge your brain in the right direction again.

Regain your strength by retiring your excuses, as the unhealthy mind will always try to take you out of the game.

## Psychological Factors

*Cognitive Flexibility*

The ability to adaptively adjust one's thoughts, beliefs, and behaviors in response to changing circumstances is essential for resilience. The ability to be flexible is what trains your brain to solve problems faster by thinking about them from different angles instead of continuously headbutting into the problematic wall ahead, while keeping your emotions in check.[23,24] The mind is an untamed monkey, it will keep swinging from one branch to the other constantly distracted by everything. It will not stop until and unless you give it direction and a rewarding purpose for heading in that direction. Gaining control of your mind and your nervous system is perhaps the best gift you can give to yourself and your loved ones, and you do this by making choices that align with your well-being.

Making good choices involves taking ownership of yourself, your actions, and your life.

The more you give in to short-term gratification, the shorter your span of well-being gets. If you can focus on the information, thoughts, feelings, and actions that are currently relevant to your goal, while inhibiting information that is not relevant, you are practicing cognitive control. If you avoid making choices or constantly blame others for your choices, you are essentially avoiding taking control of your brain. So, it's a conscious choice you make to stick to your ambition and self-care practice regardless of circumstances to win this game long term while loving the journey.

*Emotional regulation*

Emotions are like the tides of an ocean, there is always a natural ebb and flow. There is a high tide and a low tide, but these are regulated by the moon and the Earth's movement itself. Your emotions also need to be regulated by how you choose to move through life. If you block them, the higher they will rise and the more disastrous they will be. Regulation of emotions is the process of dictating which emotions one has when they have them, and how one experiences or expresses them. Research on children exposed to adverse childhood experiences has found that those who develop effective emotion regulation strategies, such as mindfulness or cognitive reappraisal, are more resilient and show fewer emotional and behavioral problems later in life.[25,26] Mindfulness is simply the mind being fully occupied by the present moment. It involves being detached enough to observe everything the present moment has to offer rather than fixating on one specific thing.

Cognitive reappraisal is a form of emotional regulation that involves changing how we perceive a situation's meaning or relevance to change the emotional impact of it. The way someone views and engages with the world will decide how calm or nasty their emotions will get, and the person they end up becoming over time. When you attach way too much meaning to a desire, event, or person, your emotions will get turbulent every time there is even a minor obstacle in your way. Some of us become emotional addicts, where our bodies get addicted to drama because pain and negative emotions release dopamine and endorphins to make us feel better.[27-29] Instead of having a desirable circumstance to take pleasure in, we can end up seeking pleasure from undesirable circumstances, while wondering why we end up in the same situation over and over again.

*Sense of Purpose*

Having a sense of purpose or meaning in life can provide motivation and resilience during challenging times. Both animals and humans may exhibit greater resilience when they feel a sense of purpose or connection to something larger than themselves.

Strong social connections and supportive relationships can buffer the effects of stress and promote resilience.[30] Animals and humans who have access to social support networks are often better equipped to cope with adversity and recover from setbacks. Secure attachment bonds, formed through close relationships with caregivers or peers, contribute to resilience by providing a sense of safety and security. Animals and humans living in cohesive communities often receive collective support that bolsters their ability to withstand adversity. People deeply long to belong to something bigger than themselves.

---

*"Every day we have plenty of opportunities to get angry, stressed or offended. But what you're doing when you indulge these negative emotions is giving something outside yourself power over your happiness. You can choose to not let little things upset you."*

*— Joel Osteen*

---

*Opportunities for Learning and Growth*
The environment stimulates a young brain in many ways. Exposure to different perspectives and places, guidance from a mentor, learning from experience, and having a supportive community give rise to a more aware and emotionally stable individual. Contrast this with

today's scenario of children being planted in front of TV screens and phones for hours on end, numbing their brains and halting their cognitive development.[31,32] Artificial intelligence is being fed more data. We enhance and allow algorithms to evolve, but fail to continuously upgrade and evolve our own brains which are running on autopilot.[33] Your learning does not stop with your school or degree. Both animals and humans benefit from environments that support ongoing learning and growth, which increase your capacity to deal with challenges as they emerge.[30,34,35]

For example, dogs that are not taken for regular walks not only become anti-social but also dull as sniffing diverse scents is essential for their well-being, positive feelings, and mental stimulation.[36] Similarly, people who isolate themselves from learning and exploring will find it hard to develop strategies to overcome their problems, ultimately leading to an emotional spiral of fear and worry. However, if you train your mind to constantly learn and enjoy the process of exploration, you will gain the necessary information to make the right choices and the belief that a solution can be found. The more you keep evolving through learning and overcoming your fears, the less power unpredictable change has over you.

The interplay between these factors is complex, and resilience often emerges from the dynamic interaction of all the above factors. Therefore, it's for you to check which factor/pattern has had the most impact on you. Once you know that, you will have a better clue of what has been holding you back from becoming more stable and successful and make the necessary shifts. In the next chapter, let us go through the 8 major domains that govern your internal endurance and power, deciding how unshakeable you really are in life.

But before we do, we need to discuss the core of being resilient —the human heart.

## Heart's rhythm

One of the most important factors of resilience is the heart. The heart is one of the most powerful organs in the human body. It pumps blood tirelessly throughout life, pushing around 2,000 gallons per day without rest, and can beat over 3 billion times in a lifetime. Unlike other muscles, the heart never tires as long as it's healthy. Its sheer stamina is unmatched by any other part of the body.[37,38] Imagine running a marathon continuously throughout your life—that's essentially what the heart is doing. What's remarkable is that the heart can function independently of the brain, thanks to its internal pacemaker—the *sinoatrial node*. This intrinsic electrical system makes sure the heart keeps beating, even when the brain is not directly controlling it.

The sympathetic nervous system handles the body's "fight-or-flight" response, triggering rapid heartbeats when we experience stress or danger. In contrast, the *parasympathetic* system—often called the "rest and digest" system—slows down the heart, bringing calm and balance. During times of stress, shallow breathing and an overactive sympathetic nervous system make the heart work harder, increasing the heart rate and constricting blood vessels. This constant state of alertness damages the heart over time, leading to hypertension and increasing the risk of cardiovascular disease.[39]

What's truly fascinating is the heart's ability to communicate with the brain. The heart contains over 40,000 neurons, forming what's called the *heart-brain connection*. In fact, the heart sends more signals to the brain than the brain sends to the heart, affecting emotional regulation, decision-making, and even cognitive function.[40,41] This is why heart-centered practices like slow breathing and focusing on gratitude can help balance the nervous system, lowering stress and elevating calmness.[42–46] Think of the heart as the wise elder that guides the restless mind. While the brain analyzes and breaks things down, the heart synthesizes and gives us a sense of coherence and meaning. When the heart and brain are in harmony, we experience a state called *heart coherence*, which leads to a perfect trifecta of mental, emotional, and physical health.

Both the brain and heart are run by electrical currents that produce magnetic fields. The human heart's magnetic field, although tiny, is the strongest electromagnetic field generated by the body, far more powerful than the brain's.[47,48] Changes in this field and heart rhythms occur upon activation of specific emotional states.

Heart rate variability (HRV) is the slight fluctuation in the time interval between your heartbeats and is a profound marker of internal well-being. A high HRV improves a person's emotional regulation and has been linked to higher cognitive and social abilities.[49] HRV is not just a marker of good health but also a facilitator of good decisions.[50] This HRV is influenced by the parasympathetic nervous system which is responsible for relaxing the body and creating a feeling of contentment. Someone with high HRV is likely to adapt to changes in their life, as HRV helps in generating useful responses and inhibiting impulsive and inappropriate ones.[51] Whereas a person with low HRV is likely to crumble under the pressure of uncertainty, due to improper functioning of the central autonomic network of the nervous system.

Interestingly, being able to survive pain and experiencing growth after a traumatic incident increases the HRV (making the heart more resilient).[52] Just as our heartbeat races and speeds down based on our emotions, the HRV fluctuates based on emotional states. HRV is higher when you are amused as compared to when you are fearful and angry.[53] Fear seems to be a much worse emotion than anger, as anger seemed to be associated with higher HRV than fear.[53] Basically, your heart acts like a radio tower, constantly broadcasting signals to the world around you. When you focus on positive emotions, your "signal" becomes stronger, building your capacity to invite and have positive experiences and deeper connections.

Look at the most iconic postures like the *Titanic pose* or *Shahrukh Khan's signature pose*—both involve spreading the arms wide and expanding the chest, symbolizing openness and vulnerability. When we physically open our chest, we are also expanding our heart, both emotionally and physically. These gestures, while simple, have a profound psychological impact and are like opening a door to your heart.[54-56] When the door is closed, nothing comes in or goes out. But when you open it wide, you allow love, opportunities, and positive energy to flow in. They signal to the world (and to ourselves) that we are ready to receive love, connection, and life experiences. Many gym exercises, like chest presses or flies, are designed to expand the chest and strengthen the muscles surrounding the heart. By engaging in these exercises, you are not only building physical strength but also opening up the body's emotional center. These movements improve posture, enhance lung capacity, and increase confidence, as they align with the body's natural mechanics for openness. Unfurling a sail would be another analogy for this phenomenon of the heart. The wider you open it, the more wind (opportunities, love, and connection) you can catch, propelling you forward in life with greater ease.

The word *courage* comes from the Latin word "cor," meaning *heart*. True courage is heart-centered—it's about being open, vulnerable, and ready to embrace both the joys and pains of life. When we open our hearts physically and emotionally, we build both inner strength and the ability to connect more deeply with others. By expanding your chest, spreading your arms, and opening your heart, you are not just exercising your body—you are cultivating an openness to life's experiences, building resilience, and allowing love to flow freely.

Your breath is one of the most, if not the most important indicator of your capacity for life. To increase HRV you must increase your breathing capacity. Slow breathing has been shown to stabilize $CO_2$ levels, reduce inflammatory markers, lower blood pressure, and balance blood pH, promoting relaxation and health.[57] This makes practices like mindful breathing crucial for restoring physiological balance and preventing illness.

**Actionable point:** Set 15 minutes aside every day to slow down your breath as much as possible. Remind yourself to breathe slowly. Let your exhales be longer than your inhales. You can also close your right nostril with your thumb and breathe only from the left nostril for a few minutes to relax further.

# CHAPTER 6

# Assessing Resilience

Navigating through life often seems like a constant battle of finding the right coping techniques. On one hand, they can be helpful in managing everyday stressors and challenges. But they can also be harmful if not used effectively. And then there's resilience; the ultimate goal of adapting well to life's changes. It sounds so simple, but it's easier said than done. Your coping strategies can end up destroying you more often than saving you. "Am I falling into the trap of avoidant coping?" is a question worth asking at this point. Who does not want to binge-watch shows or party away the stress? But what is the point if it's going to keep showing up again and again and again, each time making you feel more frustrated than when it first showed up? Maybe it's time to try a different approach to handling life.

Only when you truly know where you stand will you understand where you need to go. This questionnaire is meant to give you that reality check and insight.

1) What is your dominant emotion that frequently comes up throughout the day?

2) Do you feel you are unlucky?

3) How many triggers do you have? How often do you get triggered?

4) Do you tend to self-sabotage? If yes, how so? What is your primary longstanding fear? What advice would you give to a young kid who is going through this fear?

5) Do you often take the advice you are giving to others?

6) What is your primary coping mechanism? Is it all good or does it have drawbacks?

7) Do you ask yourself enough empowering questions?

8) How do you feel about randomness (in situations, people, things, etc.)?

# 1. Your Dominant Emotions

You are most likely feeling something or the other at any point in time. We are emotional beings. Therefore, 90% of an average day in our lives is spent experiencing some form of emotion.[58] This, however, can vastly differ from one individual to another. For an increasingly stressed-out society that is witnessing spikes in depression rates, emotional numbing is a natural consequence. We shut down our ability to experience a positive and negative emotion to protect us from further trauma. In this situation, a person may undergo far fewer emotions than needed as well. Emotions have a bad reputation for messing with our lives and making them more complicated. This is a fallacy. Emotions are enablers that will allow you to feel like life is a boon or a bane depending upon which emotion is dominant in your body.

If we were to explain the role of thoughts and feelings, we can take the analogy of creating a drawing. You have a piece of blank paper in front of you, and you are sitting with a pen or a pencil. You first trace the margins and the outlines of what you want, and then you add the details, shade it, or color it. Our thoughts are like the outlines of any drawing/idea we have in our brain. They are present to give structure and order to your idea, defining all the elements in your drawing. As remarkable as thoughts can be, they fall flat without emotions, as it's the emotions that represent the different colors and shades of life, adding more depth and meaning. This is how out of the thousands of thoughts racing through our brains, some get elevated by emotion and projected onto our brains as a vision, making it a lived experience.

Without emotions, everything would look like more of the same thing, robbing you of the drive to be inspired and create something new. Positive emotions are an incentive for your body to remain healthy and grow.[54] Negative emotions stemming from hopelessness and distrust signal the body to stop growing and eventually start self-destructing.[59,60] This does not mean that there is no place for sadness or other difficult emotions in your life; they are very important as they are potent indicators of change. They can push you out of your comfort zone and make you seek for more in life, furthering your evolution.

Dissatisfaction is a powerful avenue for creation. Every successful business thrives and prospers upon first identifying a gap in the market and then filling it with its unique strategy. This is quite similar to how our emotions work as well. The negative emotions are simply calling your attention to a lack of something important and pushing you to be more creative in solving it. Every negative emotion or experience is an opportunity to evolve, quite similar to a trampoline. You step onto a trampoline, and you first go down. It's that mass and gravity of going down that sets the momentum for you to be propelled upwards. The only condition is you must allow yourself to be lifted upwards. If you keep endlessly pressuring yourself, you will only go down, ripping through the buoyant fabric that is there to support you.

Going through sadness only deepens your capacity to experience more profound happiness with authenticity. Sadness feels like it's hollowing you out; however, you can also say it's adding more depth to you. The meaning is the same but the perspective and feeling you get from using each of these words is very different. You cannot know true happiness with sadness, day without night, healing without pain, love without hate, and strength without weakness. The contrast/duality/polarity whatever you want to call it exists solely for this reason. It is there to help you understand what you really want and to make you experience it as fully and deeply as you desire. The only thing needed to go from one pole to the other is trust. This is why living in a broke and broken world that is devoid of trust is absolutely maddening. The only way back is to start trusting. Trust yourself first. Trust yourself to make better choices and decisions. Trust the deep-seated desires you have. Trust the love you hold for yourself and the unified force that has created everything including you.

If God/the universe has created hell then it has also created heaven on earth. So, you being a child and extension of this source can also be forgiven for the pain and mess you have created while being celebrated for the joy and brilliance you put out into the world.

Every positive emotion is a celebration of your evolution. Our feelings are not the overrated and annoying side effects of living, instead they are the essence and gift of being human. Your emotions have been pre-programmed upon birth and shaped by the experiences you have had growing up. They continue to be influenced by some powerful experiences you have as an adult. Very rarely do we consciously choose and direct our emotions the way we like them, because we are too busy trying to run away from them or bury them with food cravings, impulsive shopping, and binging media content. All these are unconscious ways to self-soothe that do not actually heal the underlying wounds.

The answer to taming your emotions is not to shame yourself for experiencing a particular emotion, but it starts with accepting your current emotion and selecting the next one that is more conducive to your well-being. There is an exercise we will learn in the later chapters that will help you transition from spiraling out of control to spinning into healthy control.

Before that, close your eyes, try to remember the past week's events, and observe the expression or feeling you had in those memories. Was it angry, anxious, calm, or happy? How we interpret and react to situations is closely linked to the default emotion we feel most of the time, as emotions act as filters to our lens of perception. Your dominant emotional state (DES) dictates your behavior as well.[61-63] Each DES has a chemical signature that shows up as the cocktail of hormones released in the body that we perceive as an emotion. Say you successfully finished a project but a few things went wrong. A happy individual is likely to fixate on the things that went right while an angry individual is likely to fixate on the things that did not work out and find a reason to throw a tantrum instead. A calm individual may be able to appreciate the win and provide constructive feedback. The success of the project is then subjective based upon the perceiver's viewpoint influenced by their emotional state.

Your brain and body remember this default emotion, and use it as the first reaction to most situations, even when there might be another more appropriate emotion. This is why sometimes it seems like people are overreacting. They have the same heightened response to every small or big circumstance, as it's a learned behavior that is asking to be changed for the better (they just don't know it yet).

So, don't hide behind the façade of "I am fine" and really ask yourself what you are feeling most of the time. Identify the top three predominant emotions and see if you are happy with them. If not, what do you want to change them to?

Note down the frequency of the emotions you go through (mostly/sometimes/rarely). Here is a list of emotions for you to choose from in case you have not felt a different emotion in a while:

| Emotional State | Frequency (Mostly/Sometimes/Rarely) |
| --- | --- |
| Blissful | |
| Peaceful | |
| Joyful | |
| Loved | |
| Adored | |
| Admired | |
| Appreciated | |
| Amused | |
| Calm | |
| Courageous | |
| Accepted | |
| Neutral | |
| Awkward | |
| Bored | |
| Craving | |

| | |
|---|---|
| **Confused** | |
| **Anxious** | |
| **Sad** | |
| **Melancholic** | |
| **Disgusted** | |
| **Angry** | |
| **Envious** | |
| **Insecure** | |
| **Guilty** | |
| **Shameful** | |
| **Fearful** | |

If you still are not sure about your DES, perhaps the dominant state is that of uncertainty, doubt, or erraticity. Look at the primary/first emotion that comes up when you approach the things that matter to you. You can recall the most prominent parts of the week and identify the emotion you were experiencing.

Experiencing an emotion is different from becoming an emotion. We unintentionally end up associating with an emotion and making it our identity when we say:

I am sad.

I am annoyed.

I am scared.

I am happy.

The first three examples are not emotions that you would like to carry forward with you I am guessing, so be careful when you place them after I am. Whatever you place after "I Am" becomes your state of being in the short term and your identity in the long run upon repetition. This doesn't mean you don't acknowledge your emotions, because that would be denial and suppression of feelings that will suddenly stir up a storm later on. When you say I am feeling "_____", you are acknowledging and releasing what you are feeling without making it your identity.

**Actionable point:** To shift your DES, you need to acknowledge the state you are in and the state you are moving towards. When you are in a deep negative state of mind, highly positive emotions will just not resonate. They will most likely feel false and make you think you are kidding yourself. So instead of trying to leap into the abyss, gently guiding yourself back towards joy by taking one small step towards the next best emotion is a better strategy. You can do that by saying the following to yourself 3 or more times when you become aware of your emotions:

- ❖ Even though I have been a/an --------
  person, I am now becoming a/an ---------
  person

Or

- ❖ Even though I have felt --------, I am now
  choosing to feel ---------

The emotions that you experience most often are your primary emotions. The emotions you experience sometimes are your secondary emotions, and the ones you rarely feel are tertiary. It's up to you to promote or demote these emotions among tertiary, secondary, and primary grades by conscious choice and acceptance.

# 2. Perception of Luck

Who does not want to be lucky? Everybody right? Not really. Some may not want to be lucky or come across as lucky. You see, luck is a big crutch people use to make sense of some stellar achievements or turn of events because it seems too good to be possible. In doing so, however, it strips away the individual's role in creating that luck. Remember the hero's journey of struggle and upheaval? Where is the evolution, growth, setbacks, being the underdog, and then the magnificent rise? Luck can dampen the significance of the win, so some may just feel offended when their effort is reduced to luck. You will only believe what you have seen evidence of in your experience so far. When we have seen a lot of struggles around us, accepting that good things can just happen with ease seems improbable. This can leave us wondering if that luck will strike again, or if it was just a rare miracle. What is worse is that luck can sometimes trigger us into feeling like imposters.

- "I just got lucky with this job, but will I get it again if I need it?"
- "I just got lucky with this person. What will I do if they leave?"
- "Did I really deserve it? Or did I just get lucky?"
- "Would someone else who worked harder be more worthy of receiving this luck?"
- "Did I do enough?"
- "Am I good enough for this?"
- "Am I worthy of receiving this when there are so many in need?"

When we think linearly, luck does not add up and can even make life seem unfair. That is why people look at others and feel envious or insecure. There is an element of judgment involved in the receiver's worthiness. This judgment only weighs you down and further alienates you from the potential of luck. As you sow, so shall you reap, right? Yes, but you don't reap the very minute or the next day of sowing. Some seeds sprout overnight while some take years. Similarly, sometimes you get lucky in some aspects of your life rather quickly, while others take years on end. Luck is not always linear.

Imagine you're at a professional conference and you decide to strike up a conversation with someone standing next to you during a coffee break. Your interaction doesn't come with any specific expectations; you chat for a few minutes, exchange contact information, and then go about the rest of the conference. You think little of it afterward. Several months later, you find yourself looking for new job opportunities. You remember the person you met at the conference and decided to reach out. To your surprise, not only is their company hiring, but they also remember you fondly and put in a good word for you with the hiring manager. This leads to an interview and eventually a job offer at a company you hadn't even considered before. In this example, the initial act of friendly networking at the conference doesn't have an immediate, tangible benefit. It was a small, seemingly insignificant event. However, the positive impression you made turned into a significant career opportunity down the line.

By simply engaging in friendly conversation, you sowed a seed of goodwill. Months later, you reaped the benefits in an unexpected and substantial way—a new job opportunity that might not have been available to you otherwise. Our actions can have far-reaching effects we cannot foresee at the moment. The non-linear nature of luck means that small actions today can lead to big, unpredictable outcomes in the future. Therefore, it's often beneficial to approach life with a mindset of generosity and openness, as you can never predict how or when your actions will come back to benefit you.

What does creating your luck mean? Does it mean working very hard until what you want eventually shows up? No, that's not luck. That is receiving the fruit of your work. Luck entails something that happens with minimal effort when the person simply shows up to receive it. Lucky people show up consistently and believe that multiple good things can happen to them wherever they go. The brain always needs an incentive.[64] If it thinks that the world is a hopeless place and the past has shown that you never win, you will not expend your energy turning up at places and taking opportunities where potentially lucky incidents occur. For example, most people work hard for money. If they did not have to worry about money, how many of them would still go out and look for meaningful work to be engaged in? How many would show up at their company for work if they found out or thought that their company could not pay their full salary from now onwards?

Your perception of yourself, your life, people, and the circumstances you find yourself in are what determines your ability to create luck. Covid-19 caused a major upheaval around the world. A lot of people lost precious lives, livelihoods, freedom, and more. However, it was also during the pandemic in 2021 that a record number of 493 people became billionaires, which means a new billionaire emerged every 17 hours.[65,66] Of these, 84% of them were self-made billionaires who founded their companies and were not heirs to a throne.[66] About 40 people became billionaires by directly profiting from the fight against Covid-19.[67] This data is not meant to make you feel that you are unlucky, rather it's to show you that even amid destruction, creation and progress continue for those who pursue them.

Stop dismissing other people's success as just luck. If you do that to someone, chances are someone will take a cursory look at your achievements and write it off as luck, without acknowledging your consistent efforts behind it. What goes around will come back around.

Imagine a field of wildflowers. A bee visits a flower to collect nectar. The bee then randomly flies to another flower, perhaps miles away, to collect more nectar. Some of the pollen from the first flower gets transferred to the second flower's stigma. The second flower is now fertilized and can produce seeds. Depending on how they are dispersed, these seeds may grow into new plants, sometimes far from the original plant. The new plants provide food and habitat for other organisms, stabilize the soil, support a variety of insects, and attract other pollinators, creating a positive feedback loop. The bee just wanted nectar, but in fulfilling its desire, it helped an entire ecosystem. Also, now the bee has more flowers to source nectar from. This again illustrates the non-linear nature of luck, where small, seemingly insignificant actions can lead to significant and widespread positive outcomes in the future. Your habits, routines, mental diet, social interactions, and something as simple as smiling are all examples of this. It may seem like nothing at the moment, but it's a large vessel of success in the making. I have used the word luck a lot now, but is it all just luck or is it an intention?

Back to the analogy. The flowers have a clear intention of attracting pollinators, which is a form of investment in their reproduction. The bee is just the facilitator who comes and carries this process along, unknowingly playing a crucial role in the plant's propagation. People we attract and invite into our lives resemble these bees. They may come in with a certain intention to meet your survival needs but end up catalyzing a lot of changes in your life, fueling your growth. We also end up playing the same role as a bee in someone's else growth and their blossoming journey. This begs the question; what strategy are you using to attract and invite people? The strategy you use and the value you put out into the world will determine if you end up allowing conducive symbiotic agents like bees to enter your life or letting invasive weeds and other undesirable agents take control.

A strong association or relationship does not end with the people involved. It flourishes, it creates a space for a home, a community, and an empire. Whether that is a romantic or a business partnership; love, respect, trust, and mutual well-being will always be the bedrock of that long-lasting success.

Life unfolds in complex, often unpredictable ways, showing how interconnected and non-linear our paths can be. It's up to you if you want to wait for "luck" or just create it by adding strategic value. The right strategy will show up when the intention set is strong and grounded. An intention is not just a random goal or wish but a clear and specific declaration of what you want to invite into your life. People lack clarity in life because they are often unaware of what actually matters to them the most and what they intend to witness in their lives. Intentions help you decide and prioritize your actions based on what you value the most.

To understand your true intentions, you must first look at your needs.

- What is your primary need?
- What is your secondary need?
- What is your tertiary need?
- How often are your needs met? This will reflect the state you are in.
- How often are your needs met by yourself? Indicates your self-dependence.
- How often are you meeting the needs of others? Indicates social-cohesion.

Based on your answers to the above questions, you would have understood what matters the most right now and what should matter more to you in your life. For each need you identified, you can set an intention for it in the following way:

- ❖ I am now taking care of myself by prioritizing my need for ----------.
- ❖ I am actively seeking and creating moments that bring joy into my life.
- ❖ I acknowledge and appreciate how well my needs are met and how I am able to help others with ease.
- ❖ I intend to build and maintain meaningful relationships, fulfilling my need for ---------.
- ❖ I choose to be bigger than the sum of my needs as my resources continuously amplify and bring fulfillment.
- ❖ I naturally stay in a state of abundance and creation.

You are free to construct a sentence of your own that feels natural to you. The above intentions are examples that commonly suit us and will help you direct your attention better.

Sight is the ability to see the physical world, while vision is the gift of seeing beyond it. When you set an intention, you are setting a vision in place before it happens. Regularly remind yourself of your intentions. Especially when you feel you are going off track. The more you revisit your intentions, the deeper they become ingrained in your psyche. When your psyche changes, the way you see things and the way you do things changes. This inevitably changes the results you experience in life. You must have a roadmap before you get on the road. Most people wake up, go about the day, and then try to diffuse or change unfavorable situations that suddenly arise, only to get stressed.

By setting an intention first thing in the morning, you are charting a roadmap for how you want to live your life and making a conscious commitment to honor those intentions every day. Once you have these specific intentions in mind, then you will get a fair idea of the habits you want to pick up, the clothes you want to wear, the people you want to surround yourself with, the type and quality of work you want to do, and so on. Life is one hell of a ride with lots to offer, so make it more intentional and less accidental.

**Actionable point:** Set clear and strong intentions for each day. To remind yourself of them often, you can write them down, repeat them aloud or in your head, create sticky notes, or have a digital wallpaper of them.

## 3. Trigger Traps

How do you save a life? Protecting it is one way, and the other is by remembering its value and purpose. However, our psyche gets heavy with all the pain, chaos, rejection, discrimination, and neglect we experience while being open-minded and starts closing down all the windows of light. What we get is a person trapped by their protection system, stuck in the same place, living the same day like a loop. The value of such a life seems very little because nothing is being added, learned, explored, and experienced. In such a scenario, everything just comes with the burden of maintaining with no meaning. Change both excites and frightens us. As subtle or drastic as change can be, it's needed, as it signals growth in a new direction. Without change, there is no growth. When you don't change, your life does not change, and you lose hope. When you lose hope, your willpower and capacity to change further plummets. This is the trap most of us fall into when we accumulate several triggers in our lifetime without actually improving or eliminating them.

Staying away from triggers, nestled in your comfort zone, keeps you safe, but it also keeps you stunted. Then what is the solution? Just expose ourselves to triggers and get agitated all the time to build our resilience to them? Not quite. Let us take the example of a container made of iron, and fire some bullets at it. What is the outcome? The bullets can pass through. The same container smelted into steel becomes much more capable of blocking bullets. The triggers i.e., the bullets—haven't changed, but the stuff you, the container, are made of has been alchemized into something much more powerful. The only thing to change in this world is the self. No one, or nothing else. You can use fear, anger, manipulation, and physical pressure to force a change around you, but nothing is as light, seamless, powerful, and lasting as changing yourself.

People don't like to hear that. "Why should I change myself if that person has so many issues and is hurting so many people? Why should that onus be on me? I am a good person and I don't deserve it." No one deserves pain, hurt, or suffering. However, what we fail to understand is that everything we do, everything we say, and everything we choose, has consequences. If life was like an interactive web series, it would present us with mundane or difficult scenarios, and play out the storyline based on what we choose.

But wait, that is exactly what it does. At every turn, life will continue to present us with options. If you have made a couple of wrong turns before, you will still get a chance to make the right one, if you keep your eyes peeled for it, intending to find it. If you keep acting the same way, making the same choices, nothing new is going to come out of life. You will never have all the answers before you take a step and make a choice. You just have to make the best of what you have and not repeat the ways that haven't worked. After all, insanity is doing the same thing over and over again and expecting different results, right? If you view every present moment as a chance to make a choice, a better choice than you have made so far, you and your life will start changing at a turbo-charged pace.

How many triggers do you have? How often do you get triggered?

Here's a quiz to assess mental and emotional resilience. Answer each question and tally your score of A's, B's, and C's at the end to see your resilience level.

**Instructions**: Choose the option that best describes how you feel or behave.

1. **When faced with a challenge, I:**

   A) Feel overwhelmed and anxious

   B) Take a deep breath and start problem-solving

   C) Feel confident in finding a solution

2. **In stressful situations, I:**

   A) Withdraw or avoid and get agitated

   B) Seek support from friends or family

   C) Stay calm and focused

3. **When receiving criticism, I:**

A) Feel hurt and dwell on it

B) Consider the feedback and try to improve

C) Appreciate it as an opportunity to learn

4. **How do you view failures?**

A) As a reflection of my inadequacy

B) As a learning experience

C) As stepping stones to success

5. **When something unexpected happens, I:**

A) Panic and feel out of control

B) Take it one step at a time

C) Adapt quickly and find solutions

6. **My problem-solving skills are:**

A) Poor; I often feel stuck

B) Adequate; I find solutions eventually

C) Strong; I approach problems proactively

7.  **In relationships, I am:**

    A) Often insecure and dependent

    B) Supportive and open to communication

    C) Confident and resilient, even in conflict

8.  **When dealing with negative emotions, I:**

    A) Let them take over

    B) Acknowledge them and seek balance

    C) Manage them effectively and stay positive

9.  **My level of optimism about the future is:**

    A) Low; I often expect the worst

    B) Moderate; I try to stay hopeful

    C) High; I am generally optimistic

## RESULTS

**Mostly A's: Low Resilience**

You may struggle with challenges and stress. Focus on building a support network, practicing mindfulness, and developing problem-solving skills.

## Mostly B's: Moderate Resilience

You handle some challenges well but may benefit from strengthening your resilience skills. Continue working on stress management techniques and maintaining positive relationships.

## Mostly C's: High Resilience

You have strong resilience skills and adapt well to challenges and stress.

Keep using your effective coping strategies and support others in building their resilience.

Managing your triggers involves using anchors, reviewing, and reconstructing memories, and self-soothing processes. Positive anchors are a list of things in your environment that your senses like perceiving. This list will differ from person to person. Many of us wouldn't have even paid attention to consciously noting down what we find very appealing, but this can shift our focus to a more desired state. This can be the smell of a certain flower, or cologne, or the visual of an exotic location or a loved one.

Anchors can be divided into auditory, visual, kinesthetic, olfactory, and gustatory based on the senses.

Make a list of anchors that you can switch your focus to every time you approach a trigger:

| Senses | Positive anchors |
| --- | --- |
| Auditory | |
| Visual | |
| Kinesthetic | |
| Gustatory | |
| Olfactory | |

Stay in the anchored state until you feel better. This helps you approach your trigger in a more balanced state as your thoughts will be more supportive. However, switching your focus to positive anchors is a temporary quick fix. To make a more lasting change towards our biggest triggers, you must delve into your mental space. To completely let go of the trigger, we must address it in our emotional space as well.

Memories of the past are the ghosts that scare us away from our future. A memory is perceived data that is analyzed, organized, and stored in a particular fashion. Logically, if you ask two or three people about the same event that they experienced together, you must get the same answer. However, it's observed that the same event is recalled differently by people who experienced it at the same place and time. Here are some facts to consider about memory:

Every time you try to recollect a memory, the entire memory is erased and rewritten. What you remember is hardly ever what really happened– what you remember is the last time you remembered it.

Memories are state-dependent as well. Emotional memories are mediated by the amygdala, and the memory that resonates with your current emotions will be recalled more easily.[63,64] So, if you are angry, there will be a whole entourage of angry memories unleashed one after the other in that state, further fanning your emotional flames. And if you have, for instance, started to distrust a person in your memory since you last recalled it, it's likely to get overwritten with a new version where that person is unreliable. Because that is a more "useful" version for you now according to your brain.

Both of the above facts are connected to each other as well. When you recall something, your recollection is filtered and distorted through your emotional state. A memory, when rewritten, takes on the overtones of the dominant emotional state you are in. Even your sweet memories can turn sour after a while. Or even a bitter memory can start to seem less harsh or neutral because you see it from a different vantage point.

Eyewitnesses of the same event also give slightly different accounts.[68] Different things catch different people's eyes based on their own biases, priorities, and conditioning.

Bad memories need not be erased. Acknowledge whatever you experienced. However, these memories can be overwritten as all memories are. When we recall a hurtful memory, we indict a judgment on the people involved, labeling their personalities. Not only do we relive the memory but also amplify the hurt every time we do this. There are two ways of tackling these emotions:

Calm down, ground yourself, then view the memory not from your point of view, but from the other person's eyes or a third-party perspective as just an observer of the scene. When your vantage point changes, your view changes. You will see the memory differently from then on. BUT... This is easier said than done when the emotions associated with the event are too intense and it's hard to be detached.

This second part may ruffle some feathers but here goes. Every moment that becomes a memory is a product of people's awareness, emotions, and, as a result, their choices at the time. How many times have you wondered – "Only if I knew better, I wouldn't have done this... or I would have done this sooner". In the myriad possibilities of what could have transpired at that moment you recall, a particular choice of actions and words played out. If remembering this particular possibility is doing you more harm than good, then you can choose to reconstruct this memory differently by seeing a positive chain of events occurring instead of the negative. What words and actions of yours would you have changed and consequently, what would be the desirable change in the events that happened, or words and actions of the other people involved? What you are doing essentially is presenting yourself with a best-case scenario that could have emerged from higher awareness and better choices made in that past moment.

Every time the hurtful memory comes up, superimpose it with an alternative possibility devoid of any commentary or judgment. By remembering this alternative possibility, you are reducing the emotional charge associated with a certain memory without denying or resisting it. What this does is that it opens you up to considering different perspectives and making better choices rather than feeling unsafe, judged, and scared from a memory that is holding you hostage and preventing you from moving on with life. Train yourself to swim in an ocean of possibilities, and pick the one that serves you and everyone else in the best way, instead of looking at and recalling life as a one-way ticket to hell or heaven.

Why do different people remember the same event differently? Let us explore that more. Memory is a byproduct of three processes in the brain: encoding, storage, and retrieval.[69,70] The first step itself, i.e., encoding, is subjective as it depends upon the individual's perception, which is influenced by our past experiences and the future experiences that we expect. Our perception guides our selective focus on picking out information we find useful while excluding the rest. Storage of memories can vary depending upon the diet and sleep patterns of the individual as well.[71] Memory retrieval has even more variables involved besides health. The state of mind you are in also matters, as it's harder to recall something when you are stressed. The wording of the question that prompted the memory retrieval also can change what we recall about the event.[72,73] In one study, participants were shown car accident videos and were asked to guess the speed at which the cars were moving.[74] When asked how fast cars were moving when they "crashed" or "smashed" into each other, people judged them faster than when asked how fast they were moving when "contacted" or "hit".

In short, memory is very malleable and subject to quite a few parameters. There is no reason for you to hold on to a memory way past its expiration date stabbing your wounds. We are taught to memorize in school but we are not taught how to navigate the memories that serve us and the ones that don't. Learning does not stop at school; it's merely the beginning of what is a lifelong process. While we are in school, we are told that we have to graduate and get into a good college, then our life will be set. Then it becomes "You just have to graduate from college and crack your job interview, then your life is set." Followed by "You just have to get married and be promoted to the top post at your company, then your life is set." By this time, people are fed up still waiting around for life to "be set". Life can never be set, you can feel settled where you are, sure, but life? Life can never be set. It's meant to change and evolve, and so are you, if you really want to feel like you are living.

The whole point of life is that the old is constantly discarded and the new is simultaneously created. That is what separates you from the furniture you are sitting on, or any other inanimate object. Our body replaces about 330 billion cells daily, which accounts for 1 percent of all our cells. Hence, in 80 to 100 days, your body would have regenerated 30 trillion cells, which is the equivalent of a new you. This feature of ours is on autopilot mode. But what about mentally? What about emotionally? How long does it take for you to renew your mental and emotional paradigms? Both of which have a tremendous impact on your biological growth as well. Are you hung up on the same old hurtful memories or have you moved to create better ones to replace the old? The more you wait around for things to change, the longer you take to extract happiness out of life. The longer the refresh rate, the slower you move through life, and the more frustrating it gets to navigate it. Similar to a web browser in the early 2000s that kept hanging for days.

How can the impact of your triggers on you change if you remain the same? What perpetuates these triggers is the emotional charge associated with them and your reaction to them. Unless we break the pattern of triggers, the loop will continue to play itself out. So, the answer is to learn the lesson behind the pattern and bid farewell to the pattern forever.

*The past is history, the future is a mystery, and only in the present are you actually free.*

**Actionable point:** Keep a list of positive anchors ready. Switch your perspective to that of a third party. Revisit your hurtful triggers and create an alternative possibility of that scene if you and the people around you had a higher level of wisdom and awareness. Expand your comfort zone bit by bit by trying new things, and being open to new perspectives to understand all the different possibilities available to you.

## 4. Self-Sabotage

Not only is self-sabotage the punishment we inflict upon ourselves for our perceived failures in life, but it's also a defense mechanism for the broken. When you believe you deserve less and are not worthy, you will kick even the best opportunities out of the way, because they only increase your sense of unworthiness. The closer the good thing comes to you, the greater the contrast in worth you see between that and you, causing you to push it away and protect yourself from feeling even smaller than you already do.

Forms of self-sabotage can range from mild to dangerous. Either way, it's not a great place to be in. Self-sabotage can involve gathering a set of disempowering and dysfunctional beliefs that make us underestimate our abilities, suppress our emotions, and make us bitter or numb towards life. It may take decades to even realize that you were self-sabotaging because it happened so subtly over the years with no obvious major trigger. This is why, as adults, we may experience less joy than we did as kids. Not because we are incapable of it, but because we are ignorant of the ways happiness is inherent in us. Everyone is born as a bundle of joy, with innocence and curiosity. Look into the eyes of a child or the eyes of a pet. No words are said, yet it sparkles and brims with a feeling of being whole, complete, and perfect. However, as we grow up, we begin attaching terms and conditions to our happiness by linking it to goals, people, careers, and a host of other external objects, forever caught in the pursuit of happiness. Quite similar to desperately searching for an object all over the premises, just to realize you had it with you the whole time and just didn't bother to search within yourself for it first.

One of the key milestones in development is the ability to become self-aware, and the mirror test is classic evidence to gauge the level of self-awareness in animals and humans. How often do we as adults really look at ourselves in the mirror to explore all that we are? Even if we look in the mirror, what is the prime intention? −To fix our flaws. As we grow old, the same mirror that was once intriguing as a child becomes an avenue to beat ourselves up. So essentially, when it comes to others, we see the good and the bad depending upon our fixation on them. However, when it's about ourselves, it's usually just all the bad that needs to be fixed to be happy. Mirrors, be it actual mirrors or just people reflecting our traits, offer a wealth of information about us, making us more aware of not just the flaws but the self as a whole. Why postpone your happiness till someone comes along and compliments you about a unique feature about you? When you acknowledge it by yourself, it becomes prominent to others as well without you needing a compliment. This is not just another motivational platitude. It's ingrained in our being. To understand this phenomenon, we must discuss mirror neurons, which are the biological mirror in us.

These are a specific set of neurons that respond to behavior we notice in others by imitating it ourselves. An example of this is someone yawning, or reaching out for a sip of water, which prompts us to do the same, but it does not have to be a visual cue, it can be auditory as well. These neurons develop before the age of 12 months in humans, to help them learn behaviors from their caretakers and surroundings by observing. The Hebbian theory proposed by Donald Hebb suggests "Cells that fire together, wire together".[75] This is a cellular rendition of the saying "Birds of the same feather, flock together". When a cell is close enough to repeatedly and persistently stimulate another cell B, its synaptic strength (efficiency to activate the other) between the two increases.[76]

Similarly, on the human level, the people you consistently hang around with and the people who raise you have the power to trigger you the most and influence similar behaviors in you. These mirror neurons go beyond just imitation, they help us understand the intention of the actions, consequently predicting the next motor act of the not-yet-observed action. Empathy is another area where mirror neurons work their magic. Several studies have shown that more empathic people have stronger activations of the mirror system in terms of both hand actions and emotions, which supports the idea that empathy closely correlates with the mirror system.[77–80] The activation of the mirror neuron network allows empaths to process the intentions and feelings of other people like their own.

A few small studies have also found the opposite in psychopaths and narcissists in whom the activation of mirror neuron systems was lower while processing emotions.[81,82] The ability to explain through metaphors is also a function of the mirror neurons that can connect information from different senses and places and piece together as a coherent theory.[80] Hence, mirror neurons are crucial for the study of the self and self-related information processing.

To understand self-sabotage better, let's consider the common narcissist-empath dynamic that can play out in any relationship —personal or professional. The narcissist here is the manipulative taker who is just not satisfied and will berate and/or breadcrumb the empath enough to keep the cycle going. Unhealthy empaths are the hamsters on the wheel who are overly sensitive to the needs of others while being blind to their own. The empath by default would be considered purely as the giver, however, it's not so. In order to go above and beyond to feed the narcissist, the empath steals from their own self. They take away their own time, energy, health, wealth, aspirations, and choices to accommodate the narcissist's endless needs. The empath chases by excessively giving love/appreciation/attention to avoid rejection while the narcissist distances by solely taking love/appreciation/attention but rarely giving it to avoid rejection. Their goal is the same but their modus operandi is different. Neither of them feels whole and happy, and the only goal they achieve is covert self-sabotage while pursuing the overt goal of a harmonious connection.

---

*"The child who is not
embraced by the village will
burn it down to feel its
warmth"*

*— African proverb*

---

It would be important to note that it's completely possible for a person to be both of these characters. They may show up as a narcissist in one relationship but also show up as an empath in the primary relationship that broke them and pushed them into narcissism as a self-defense mechanism. People behave differently with different people, as each one of them mirrors a different aspect of them. It's highly possible that you display both these behaviors with yourself. One part of you is supportive and assuring whereas the other is condescending and demanding.

Either way, the only way out is to stop playing this game altogether —with yourself and with others by learning to be enough on your own and not tying your self-worth to giving and receiving. Your self-worth stops being YOUR SELF-worth the minute you attach it to anything beyond you. It becomes your circumstantial worth, which is ever fleeting and never reliable.

Self-sabotage is also a way in which you stop yourself from getting something that you don't think you are ready for. It's holding you back, hoping you don't fall flat on your face. For example, maybe you've been stopping yourself from going for your driving test, or you do go, but you don't prepare or practice, maybe because you just don't feel comfortable or confident enough to drive on the streets. We hold ourselves back a lot, even from the things we yearn for, because we don't know if we will be okay with what comes after it.

**"If I fall in love with this girl/guy, will I lose myself in them so much that I can't make decisions for myself anymore or enjoy my freedom?"**

–Runs away.

**"If I succeed, will I have to leave a lot of family and friends behind because I will have to devote time and effort towards newer social circles?"**

–Ends up aiming low.

**Or "If I fail again, will it disappoint me and my loved ones even more, so let me delay trying?"**

–The latter sounds like the nation we have all been in at some point, which is none other than procrastination.

The most common way that self-sabotage shows up in our lives is through procrastination. We procrastinate when we are anxious about the task at hand. By putting off the task, people can avoid negative emotions, even if they cannot fulfill long-term goals that would bring them happiness. The inability to believe you are capable or worthy will stop you from doing the things that are important for your growth. With every failed attempt to do the thing you want, you "prove" to yourself that you can't or shouldn't do it. It's a vicious loop that people get stuck in, forever retreating into their comfort zone, and wondering why good things don't happen to them. The desire to avoid emotional pain and protect themselves could be the reason for sabotaging a relationship. Harmful thought patterns can occur automatically without conscious processing. To uncover them, try to bring more conscious awareness to your thoughts.

One of the key reasons we feel we are not good enough is that we try to view and understand ourselves through the eyes of others. What happens when you try to view an image through two lenses of different powers and filters? You get a distorted image. Similarly, constantly worrying about what others think about us produces a misplaced sense of self. Self-sabotage can reinforce a misplaced sense of worthlessness and justify negative thoughts that have no basis in reality.

Let me offer you a metaphor instead of didactic advice here. Consider a puppeteer, holding up weighted puppets attached to him through strings. He puts on a play to explore his joy of creativity, bringing in puppets of all sizes and shapes that take the audience on an adventure. Puppetry is a form of storytelling and self-expression by communicating ideas while invoking fun and intrigue. In this quest of making the puppets dance, interact, and tell a story, the puppeteer experiences pain–pain of fatigue and pain of damage. Therefore, besides being creative, they must have strength as well to keep the puppets in action and the show running. You are the puppeteer of your life, and your desires are your puppets. Your desire is nothing without you, although you will survive even without it. You don't need your desire. Your desire needs you.

However, if you make your happiness conditional to achieving that desire, then you become the puppet controlled by the strings of your desire, unable to move without an intervention. This is the state most people are in. "I will be happy when I meet the expectations of that other person and they become happy." "I will be happy when I get that job." "I will be happy when I get that person." No. Your true happiness is unconditional. It lies in simply existing, yearning to experience life. It's always there if you choose to tap into it.

Yes, fulfilling your desires can make you realize the happiness you already hold inside. However, you do not need them if you choose to be happy right now. Happiness is not a condition;

it's a choice. You choose to make your happiness conditional by attaching them to milestones. You can also choose to make it unconditional by detaching it from everything else other than your existence and having the freedom to create your life. Having desires and pulling the strings attached to them for a long time can exhaust you, but do not let it damage you. Build your capacity and your fitness (mental, emotional, and physical), and finish what you start, as the puppeteer does for the story arc of his puppets.

So, what's the solution for self-sabotaging? Neutralize your emotional charge by understanding that you do not have to insert your self-worth and happiness into your desires. You are who you choose to be. How does the person you choose to be think, feel, and act? They do things because it's natural to them, not because they have something to prove. Embody this character. Also, really ingrain into your brain and heart the deep knowing that you are enough. No one is going to come and tell you that unless you tell it to yourself first. You must remind yourself of that fact. Even if life's circumstances may show that you are not, you must accept and allow the relief that "I am enough" brings to your mind and body. As you do this, there is no reason anymore for you to continue self-sabotaging, as whatever the challenge is, you are now enough of a solution for it. A lot of times it's when you feel you don't need more that you start receiving more in life. Similarly, when you feel and know like you are enough, you will keep finding more and more reasons and experiences that make you feel that way.

---

*"Unless you learn to face*
*your own shadows you will*
*continue to see them in others,*
*because the world outside you*
*is only a reflection of the*
*world inside you"*

*— Unknown*

---

Be impeccable with your word. What you say you will do, do it without fail. Even if it's the smallest of things, follow through on what you committed to. Do not over-commit and underperform. It will erode your faith in yourself and lead you into more self-sabotaging behavior. Your primary job is to take care of yourself first so that you can be of service to others next. By doing this you are essentially building yourself a reservoir of the world's most valuable currency — trust, with the most valuable player in your life — you. Leaving you nothing to fear because you already have everything you really need which is faith in who you are and what you can create.

**Actionable point:** Seek happiness from the smallest of things so that your happiness becomes unconditional and independent of external circumstances.

Start being enough for yourself and stop trying to be enough for other people. If you are not enough for yourself, you will never be enough for others. Follow through on your word no matter what happens. Start small and do not overcommit. Let your words become an undeniable command for yourself.

Extract 100% satisfaction from every break you take by being immersed in the present moment. Or else you will need to take 10 breaks that only fill you up by 10% each time, slowing down your momentum and ultimately reducing your drive towards your goals/tasks. Don't take a break where you do something for fun with half a mind still thinking about what needs to be done. Choose quality over quantity when it comes to taking breaks.

## 5. Listening to Your Wisdom

Why is it easier to advise others than to advise ourselves better? The answer is simple —it's your vantage point. When you advise someone, you have observed the situation from a distance as a third party and have considered multiple perspectives. However, when we are involved in a situation ourselves, it's like falling into a pit, having tunnel vision, and being unable to see a broader view of the problem. This is what happens when we take everything personally. We develop perceptual blinders. Just like a racehorse rushes to the destination, we rush in to prove our point of view and reestablish what we think is right without updating our information by observing our surroundings. This is also because the brain tries to find mental shortcuts (called heuristics) to cut down the time we spend on decision-making.

Generalizations, rule-of-thumb, and even stereotyping are examples of the heuristics we use. Getting to know an entire crowd of new people can be cumbersome, so the brain filters out people based on different stereotypes, narrowing the search but furthering prejudice. Although this saves us some time and energy, the decisions made can be more flawed as they arise out of cognitive biases, making it difficult to see alternative solutions, have new creative ideas, or meet new people.

The Solomon Paradox, named after the biblical King Solomon, reflects the phenomenon where people offer better advice to others than they do for themselves. It's easier to see the obvious solutions to problems that are not your own. Research led by Igor Grossmann from the University of Waterloo supports this concept. His studies revealed people exhibit more objective reasoning when considering other people's problems than their own. According to his data, people are 31% more likely to look at the situation from multiple perspectives when discussing others' conflicts than their own.[83,84] They are also 22% more likely to seek more information about the circumstances of others' conflict, compared to their own problems, which entail a higher degree of assumptions.[83,84]

The internal mechanism behind the Solomon Paradox involves emotional detachment. When we evaluate someone else's situation, we do so without the emotional involvement that clouds our judgment when assessing our circumstances. This detachment allows for a more balanced and rational evaluation of the situation. One practical approach to overcoming the Solomon Paradox is to adopt a third-person perspective when evaluating our problems.

Write a letter to yourself, speak or journal in the third person (He/She/Your name instead of I, me, myself). Role-playing another character talking to you can help create the necessary emotional distance to make wiser decisions. Your pants are not on fire. Even if they are, for a moment, think from another person's point of view, who may help you find the fire extinguisher. Grossman found that participants who used first-person pronouns to discuss their situation exhibited less ability to recognize the limits of their own knowledge, consider others' perspectives, and search for a compromise compared to those who spoke about their problem in the third person.[83,84] Self-distance by considering your problem as someone else's problem.

How can we give advice when our confidence in ourselves is low? Failing repeatedly while trying to achieve goals drains people's confidence in themselves. However counterintuitive it may sound, giving advice may restore it, but the caveat is to be detached from the outcome. We believe good things are possible for others, but when it's about us, we think we are unlucky and ask "Why me? Why is it always me who has to go through this?" You must go through it because it's your lesson to learn, not someone else's.

Until we reflect on our lives, we cannot understand what mistakes kept perpetuating that pattern in our lives. Giving advice helps us look back at our lives and retrieve memories to analyze them in a helpful light. Hence, in order to give advice, the advisor performs a biased search of memory where successful and productive behaviors of the past are remembered. Advisors' confidence is likely to grow because of this biased memory scan. Based on this memory, a strong intention to improve arises, and the person can come up with the appropriate next steps to be taken.[85] Not only that but confident individuals aim higher and are more likely to stay committed to putting in the required efforts over a period.

Confidence in ability is a better predictor of pursuing a goal than the ability itself. Because if you don't think you can do it, why would you even try? If you did not try, how will you know? If you did not put consistent efforts into it, how will you improve that ability? Lacking confidence in your own wisdom and ability is one way we disqualify ourselves from getting what we want. Just being asked to give advice makes you feel you are not as incompetent as you were finding yourself to be moments ago. It's an empowering place to be, which makes us feel we can put the past behind us as we have learned something and will not repeat the same mistake. This doesn't mean all advice is good advice. Constantly giving advice without stopping to pause and reflect can turn into overconfident behavior. This is why being an observer and having the mindset of a learner goes a long way in giving sound advice that does not come from a place of ego.

People love advising others because it makes them feel like a powerful and influential person.[86] However, the problem with most people is that they don't follow through on their brilliant advice. Not following through on your own advice is more sinister than you think, because you are essentially telling yourself that your words are not reliable. You do not do what you say. You do not practice what you preach and all that leaves you with is the feeling of being a hypocrite and an imposter. In order to get significant results, and please people, we tend to over-commit because — hey, words are cheap, right? Not really. When you don't do what you say you will do —Yes, your words are very cheap and not much value to yourself or others after a point in time.

Remember, I said monkey see, monkey do? If someone receiving advice from you sees you are not doing it yourself, they lose trust in you and your advice. Your advice, although great, will then fall on deaf ears. So show and tell, not just for others to believe you, but for you to believe yourself. Don't destroy the credibility of your words by promising yourself stars, but not even going outside to see them.

The thoughts and qualities we appreciate in others are often unacknowledged when they arise within us. When faced with a nerve-racking situation, take back some of that power by giving yourself advice from a third-person perspective. Giving advice can be much more powerful than receiving advice. Researchers observed this in a set of studies conducted in middle schoolers as well. When struggling students were asked to advise younger students, the simple act of sharing their insights instilled higher confidence in them, motivating them to do better than the students who received motivational advice. Strugglers who gave advice, compared with those who received expert advice, were more driven to save money, control their tempers, lose weight, and seek employment.[87]

Giving advice is an active state of mind that is more engaged in the present moment while listening is a more passive activity. This is why we tend to learn more when we teach others what we have learned. Each one of us, regardless of an IQ test, has lived life through experience and has gathered wisdom. You only need the right lens of perception to analyze the information and decipher it. In the age of the internet, people seek advice not because they lack the information, they do it because they lack the right analysis of the information they have. Everyone just wants someone to help us "get it" i.e., understand it in a way that we will never forget it.

The best way to help someone understand something is by showing them and sharing your experience rather than telling them how it works. Personal stories, reviews, and testimonials help us understand an experience and the insights that come from that lived experience. Telling someone to be better is nothing compared to showing a person what it means to be a better person because the former is just information, and the latter is perspective.

Perspective shifts your inner state of being and vice versa. When you have the perspective that every challenge is just an opportunity for growth, you are more relaxed and motivated. Similarly, when you are relaxed and motivated, you are more likely to see solutions and ideas than problems and challenges. Your perspective shapes who you are at any moment, and that is nothing more than what you are choosing to focus on and how you are choosing to analyze it in that instant.

When you advise someone from a neutral point of view, you are in a psychologically and emotionally sound state of mind that is free from wounded negativity. You are also free from any biases and judgments. When you find yourself in the same situation, however, your mind is raided by triggering thoughts and feelings that spiral you out of your center of mental gravity. A free and fresh mind is a powerful source of mental energy that can translate simple observations into profound wisdom. Decision-making gets enhanced by strong inner insights, allowing you to approach problems with clarity and creativity. In this state, you can weigh options objectively and consider various perspectives without being clouded by emotional baggage. A calm and distanced mind fosters insightful and well-thought-out solutions that are more likely to be effective and beneficial. When there is an overwhelming decision at hand, take a few deep breaths and do something non-addictive and mundane to distract yourself (doom scrolling is not the best choice here). When you come back to focus on your decision, you may find a fresh perspective or notice something you didn't before as a result of your brain quietly processing data in the background. So be bored and self-distance yourself from your string of issues by becoming the unbiased observer of events and watching how the issues resolve in ways you would not have seen coming otherwise.

**Actionable point:** Practice third-person role play to get advice.

If you want insightful answers from deeper parts of your brain, before going to sleep every night simply ask your subconscious mind a question when you are drowsy. Go to sleep and don't go searching for the answer. You can ask the same question every night until the answers show up, and they will, when you least expect it.

# 6. Coping & Hoping Quicksand

There are always going to be some bumps, accidents, and potholes along the road, but that doesn't mean you stop driving altogether. Life still carries on. So, what do you do? You just become a more aware and skilled driver while choosing better roads. All of us have faced challenging situations in our lives, and yet here we are. We made certain choices to deal with those situations, thinking it was the best or only option, only to regret some of those choices after a while.

Many individuals rely on coping mechanisms to manage stress and difficulties, believing these strategies provide relief. However, coping mechanisms often serve as temporary fixes rather than sustainable solutions, and they can inadvertently perpetuate a cycle of stress and dissatisfaction. Life is a journey filled with ups and downs, and how we navigate these fluctuations significantly impacts our overall well-being. Coping mechanisms are behaviors or mental strategies people use to manage stress and emotional discomfort. These can range from healthy practices, like exercise and meditation, to maladaptive behaviors like substance abuse or avoidance. While some coping mechanisms can provide temporary relief, they often fail to address the root causes of stress and can lead to negative long-term consequences.

For instance, engaging in retail therapy or binge-watching TV shows might distract an individual from their problems for a short while, but what happens when the distraction ends? The nightmare of reality begins all over again, making the person scramble for more distractions, creating more quicksand for you to be trapped in. These activities do not resolve the underlying issue—what is creating this quicksand? It's our inability to direct our mental, emotional, and physical energy toward a solution because we are too caught up in lending it all to the problem by ruminating on it. People who drown in quicksand are usually those who, in a state of panic, flail their arms and legs, only to dig themselves deeper into the sandpit. Worrying does not help, and neither does running. Studies have shown that avoidance-based coping strategies are associated with increased stress and poorer mental health outcomes over time. What helps is "I AM". Two simple words that carry immense potential to change your state of being.

A (accept)

I

M (modify)

You accept the situation for what it is while knowing that you can modify the outcome by making a different move. Confront the same problem from a different perspective. You cannot know where to go if you don't know where you are in the first place. Once you know where you are, you keep exploring different routes until you find the best one. However, coping mechanisms can sometimes serve to escape reality rather than confront it. This avoidance can lead to a lack of personal growth and self-awareness. Research has shown that avoidance coping is linked to higher levels of anxiety and depression. By continually escaping from challenges, people miss opportunities to develop strength, stamina, and problem-solving skills, which are crucial for long-term stress management.[88-90] Substance abuse, overeating, or excessive gambling create a vicious cycle of dependency and deteriorating health. Sure, these behaviors may provide a quick fix but often exacerbate stress and lead to additional problems like addiction, obesity, or financial troubles. This inevitably means that individuals who rely on maladaptive coping strategies are at a higher risk for chronic stress and related health issues.

Hope is an essential human trait that can inspire and motivate. However, constantly hoping for things to change without taking proactive steps can be detrimental. This passive approach can lead to disappointment and frustration when things do not improve on their own. Psychologists emphasize the importance of setting realistic goals and taking actionable steps to achieve them, as this approach fosters a sense of agency and empowerment. When people rely solely on hope, they may fall into a state of learned helplessness, where they believe they have no control over their circumstances. This passive-hoping mindset can prevent them from taking action to actually improve their situation. Research on learned helplessness has shown that individuals who feel powerless to change their circumstances are more likely to experience depression and decreased motivation.[86-88]

Coping and hoping are not always reliable and can only bring the horse to the well but cannot make it drink the water from the well. Meaningful change happens through your internal certainty and serenity toward experiences in life. Change also happens through anxiety, but the outcome is often undesirable because the focus is more on avoiding a situation rather than finding a solution that can help you evolve.

Moping and whining are common responses to stress and adversity, but they can have a drastic impact on physical and mental health, even at the cellular level. When individuals engage in chronic complaining and negative thinking, their bodies remain in a prolonged state of stress. This leads to the release of stress hormones like cortisol. Elevated cortisol levels can impair immune function, increase inflammation, and accelerate cellular aging. Epigenetic studies have also found that chronic stress and negative emotional states are associated with shorter telomeres, the protective caps on the ends of chromosomes, which are markers of cellular aging.[91,92]

Moping and whining can also affect brain health. Persistent negative thinking patterns are linked to reduced neuroplasticity, which is the brain's ability to adapt and reorganize itself. This can hinder cognitive function and increase the risk of mental health disorders like depression and anxiety. Research has shown that individuals who engage in rumination —a form of negative thinking —have higher levels of brain inflammation and are more prone to mental health issues.

Activities like painting, coloring, silent reflection, music, recreation, and reading evolve into something even more powerful when you surrender yourself to that moment without an agenda/outcome. That powerful something is nothing but the clear realization of who you are and what really matters to you. This is where your true invincible confidence comes from. This is where your strength to experience another moment of life with courage lies. It is where the words "It's all okay, you are okay" actually land and can be felt in your body. The right coping mechanisms can open the window and give you a glimpse of how amazing you truly are. However, when the night returns, the window is shut, and we forget the little moments that gave us happiness and a complete sense of being.

Becoming confident and secure as an individual is a far better strategy than coping, hoping, and moping that we resort to when things go south in our lives. This takes work and requires you to face the heat, but it's so worth it. Anyone who has made it big in life has done it with the most precious and evergreen currency of all — trust. Trust in themselves, in their purpose, or/and trust in a higher power. How do you build this unshakeable trust? Start with building your confidence, which will, over time deepen into unwavering faith in yourself.

Confidence is the foundation of resilience and effective stress management. When individuals believe in their abilities, they are more likely to take on challenges and view setbacks as opportunities for growth. Building confidence involves setting and achieving small goals, developing skills, and embracing a growth mindset. Studies exploring job-fit suitability found that individuals with higher self-efficacy, or confidence in their ability to succeed, experienced lower levels of stress and higher job satisfaction.[93,94]

Feeling secure involves creating a stable and supportive environment, both internally and externally. We are not always born into such environments. We must create them by building strong social connections, financial stability, and a sense of purpose. Research has also shown that individuals with strong social support networks are more resilient to stress and have better mental health outcomes.[95] Financial security and a clear sense of purpose contribute to overall well-being and reduce the impact of stress. Creating an environment is easier said than done. I can't plant one seed in a barren ground one day, nurture it for 2 days, and then say I have changed the environment. It's a daily practice that turns that barren land into a grassland and eventually into a forest. The environment I create for myself will dictate the weather I shall face and my ability to deal with it.

Strengthening your energy involves practices that enhance not just your body but also your mental and spiritual well-being. This can include regular exercise, mindfulness meditation, proper nutrition, and spiritual practices. You know these things already, but you don't do it because you haven't given them enough meaning. Studies have shown that regular physical activity and mindfulness meditation can significantly reduce stress levels and improve overall health. This is because these practices help you prune out the weeds in your life that are stealing your fertile space of productivity.

The Stoic philosophy emphasizes the value of focusing on what we can control and accepting what we cannot. Why is this important and why is this an anti-thesis to stress? Our brilliant but tiny mind cannot connect the dots looking forwards, it can only see the big picture and meaning of events retrospectively. Rumination produces methane in cattle and depression and anxiety in humans. A different form of rumination, I know. The point is, can you digest life's circumstances quickly and be on the move to create better circumstances for yourself? Can you live in the present moment and be aware? This practice reduces stress and enhances overall well-being by stopping rumination in its tracks and cutting through negative spirals. It trains you to shift your attention from external circumstances filled with uncertainty to internal responses arising from a sense of surety and security.

Spiritual practices, such as prayer or meditation, have been shown to enhance a sense of inner peace and resilience. But "I am not spiritual", "I don't like religion", "People don't know who the right God is" you may say. Here is the thing though, if you are alive, you have a spirit, and that makes you spiritual by sheer existence. It's not about a God in the sky making a list of who's been naughty and who's been nice. It is about a God who experiences life through you. It's about an unseen driving force that creates, maintains, and destroys continuously throughout the universe. All of which you do normally throughout your life. Your spirit is what differentiates you from a corpse. You are alive as long as your heart beats and pumps blood due to spontaneous electrical activity at the sinoatrial node called the pacemaker.[96-98] What constantly creates this atypical spontaneous electric activity in your heart and decides the exact moment to stop it? How often are you aware of this driving force? It's the spirit that makes you want to be something, do something, and experience something of value.

However, it's the practice part that differs between us, i.e., how we choose to connect to it and celebrate it. But more than anything, spirituality is awareness of the expanding self. Even if you do not believe in an anthropomorphic figure called God, you must believe that there is an ever-expanding universe and you are an inextricable part of it that is becoming aware of itself. By being "spiritual" all you are doing is becoming more of who you truly are.

Relying on coping mechanisms, constantly hoping for things to change, and moping are ineffective strategies for navigating life and eliminating stress. These approaches offer temporary relief at best and can lead to negative long-term consequences. Instead, building confidence, feeling secure, and strengthening your energy opens up doors to lasting happiness. That fulfilled feeling of "I made it" and "I am it" comes by proactively connecting with yourself and drawing on your reflective insights and those of mentors you resonate with. True resilience and inner strength come from facing challenges head-on, taking control of our lives, and nurturing our physical, mental, and spiritual health.

**Actionable point:** Close your eyes and mentally scan through every moment you lived through today from the time you woke up till now. Do this for about 10 minutes. Simply observe the moment in your mind and move on. This meditation will not only shift you out of autopilot, but also improve your focus, give you clarity, and ground you into the present moment. The more you do this, the more you realize how fleeting your emotions and circumstances are and how change is constant, while you stay stable.

Sell well to yourself. Become your best influencer by letting the improved version of you win the negotiation with your past self who wants to cope and mope.

## 7. Interrogation

People are bad at auditing. The only things we frequently audit are our finances and the problems in our lives. Time audit? Energy audit? Mental health audit? Physical fitness audit? Information consumption audit? Emotional audit? Silly how we don't audit these things, even though they are what determine the amount of money in your bank and the problems in your life. How can we audit these things then? By using the torchlight of questioning. Imagine standing in a dark room with a flashlight. When you shine it in one direction, a small part of the room becomes visible, but the rest remains hidden. As you move the flashlight around, more areas become illuminated. Similarly, questions direct our attention and broaden our understanding, revealing new possibilities and perspectives.

Questions help to guide the brain in a specific direction instead of mulling over unwanted things. Questioning is a tool that has an innate power, transcending mere curiosity. They guide our thoughts, shape our perceptions, and influence our behaviors. Asking the right questions can reveal new layers of understanding, spark inspiration, and evoke resilience. Children can't stop asking enough questions, however, when these questions are repeatedly shot down by adults around them, they develop a phobia of asking questions. This is because they have subconsciously associated asking questions with being reprimanded and rejected. As adults, it's hard for us to even come up with innovative and off-the-bat questions like kids do because it's a skill we stopped practicing and hence lost touch with completely.

A question brings a much-necessary pause to a slew of unwanted thoughts, feelings, and behaviors, helping us recalibrate our next steps. Without questions, we would all be living dreadfully boring and monotonous lives that never seem to change and never knowing our ability to come up with interesting answers. The ability to ask questions is one of the most effective ways to communicate with others and build relationships. You show interest when you ask another person a question. You allow them to express their thoughts and feelings. In return, you can respond and express your own. Researcher Arthor Aron even identified 36 questions, that help build a bond between people and even fall in love.[99,100] It creates a space for a mutual exchange of perspectives that can help you understand the other person better. Most people ask less and assume more, which is a slippery slope to tread.

We get mad when we don't have all the answers to the questions posed to us as if it's a mark against our intelligence. You don't have to know the answer right away. Your ego does not have to get hurt right away. Instead, when you choose to be more curious about the answer than more worried about your image, you can understand the situation with more nuance. Just replying to a question is not a good answer. You would rather take your time, and assess the question and the possible answers before you reply. That is intelligence not clouded by ego.

Questioning, if used correctly, can open up all kinds of doors that lead to personal and professional growth. The quality, underlying feelings, and intention behind asking are very important to make sure you get the desired outcome. Asking numerous baseless questions has the opposite effect of annoying people. Similarly, the questions we ask ourselves should elevate our minds to a more productive, empowering, and neutral state rather than taunting ourselves into a deep spiral of hopelessness.

Empowering questions are those that prompt positive thinking and action. These types of questions rewire our brain's neural pathways, fostering a more resilient and growth-oriented mindset instead of a fearful lack mindset. When we ask empowering questions, we activate the brain's prefrontal cortex, responsible for higher-order thinking and problem-solving. This activation leads to the release of neurotransmitters like dopamine and serotonin, which enhance mood and motivation. When we ask belittling questions and panic, we activate our limbic system responsible for the fight-or-flight response. Focusing on positive words and questions increases activity in the brain's frontal lobes, promoting better decision-making and emotional stability.

Empowering questions can enhance resilience by shifting our focus from problems to solutions. They nudge your brain from what we cannot change towards what we can influence and learn. Individuals who engage in positive self-questioning are more likely to develop resilience and cope better with stress.[101] For instance, instead of asking, "Why is this happening to me?"

a more empowering question would be, "What can I learn from this experience?" This shift in perspective encourages a proactive approach to challenges, fostering resilience and personal growth.

Empowering questions have the remarkable ability to tune our mental energy. Mental energy is the capacity to sustain focused attention and cognitive effort. However, mental energy, akin to physical energy, is finite and can be depleted by negative thoughts and unproductive ruminations. By asking questions that direct our thoughts toward positive and constructive outcomes, we can conserve and enhance our mental energy. Why? Because it gives us something to look forward to, excites us, and strengthens our drive to get things done. Consider the analogy of a radio tuner. Our mind, like a radio, can pick up various frequencies of thought. Negative, disempowering questions are akin to static and interference, draining our mental energy. Asking empowering questions is like tuning into a clear, uplifting station that energizes and motivates us.

Asking questions like "What is my purpose?" or "What are my priorities?" can help clarify our goals and align our actions with our values. The University of Rochester's Human Motivation Research Group found that individuals who set clear goals and ask themselves purposeful questions are more likely to experience intrinsic motivation and sustained mental energy.[102] This alignment of mental energy with personal values and goals makes you more productive and enhances your overall well-being.

Emotional fluctuations are a natural part of the human experience. However, unchecked, they can lead to emotional distress and instability. Empowering self-reflective questions can help harmonize these fluctuations by promoting emotional awareness and regulation. For example, asking, "What am I feeling right now?" or "What do I need to feel better?" can help identify and address emotional needs. Individuals who view challenges as learning opportunities are more likely to succeed in various domains of life.[103]

*Core Questions for a Growth Mindset*

To orient the mind towards a growth mindset, raise confidence, increase faith, and spark inspiration, consider these five core questions:

1. What can I learn from this challenge/person/memory/event?

— To encourage a learning perspective, fostering growth and resilience.

2. What strengths can I leverage to overcome this obstacle?

— To build confidence by focusing on personal strengths and resources.

3. What small step can I take today towards my goal?

— To promote action and progress, enhancing motivation and faith in oneself.

4. How can I turn this setback into an opportunity?

— To shift perspective from negativity to possibility, sparking inspiration.

5. Who can I reach out to for support and guidance?

— To emphasize the importance of community, collaboration, and a growth mindset.

The power of questions extends beyond the realms of psychology and neuroscience into spirituality and philosophy. Socrates, the ancient Greek philosopher, famously employed the Socratic method, which is creating a cooperative and argumentative dialogue to stimulate critical thinking and illuminate ideas. Win the negotiation with your old self that is not letting you move forward. This method underscores the importance of asking deep, reflective questions to achieve greater wisdom and understanding. From a spiritual perspective, many traditions emphasize the significance of self-inquiry. In Buddhism, for example, practitioners are encouraged to ask questions that lead to deeper self-awareness and enlightenment. The practice of mindfulness, which involves observing one's thoughts and feelings without judgment, often begins with questions like, "What is happening in this moment?" This reflective inquiry brings your attention back to you and detaches you from all the hypothetical fires you are trying to put off in your brain.

The practice of self-inquiry, as advocated by spiritual teachers like Ramana Maharshi, involves asking questions like "Who am I?" to delve deeper into the nature of the self and achieve spiritual awakening. This process of self-inquiry is not about finding definitive answers, but about engaging in a continuous exploration that deepens our understanding and connection to the divine. It underscores the idea that the journey of questioning is itself a spiritual practice, leading to greater self-awareness and inner peace.

Questions can evoke a philosophical depth in a person's perspective, leading to existential insights and a deeper understanding of our place in the universe. They compel us to confront the fundamental aspects of our existence, such as purpose, meaning, and identity. This depth is exemplified in the philosophical inquiries of influential thinkers like Descartes, who famously asked, "What can I know for certain?" leading to his foundational conclusion, "I think, therefore I am." Questions can bridge the gap between our inner and outer worlds, helping us reconcile our personal experiences with the larger reality. For instance, asking "What is the nature of reality?" or "What is my role in the world?" can lead to profound reflections that shape our worldview and guide our actions.

Ask. By asking empowering questions, we get a shot at rewiring our brains, tuning our mental energy, and harmonizing our emotional fluctuations. The next step is to follow through with the intuitive answers and do your best.

In the quiet of the night, a whisper in the dark,
A question forms, a gentle spark.
It lights the path we cannot see,
Unlocks the door to what could be.

A query born of pure intent,
A guiding star, a message sent.
It beckons us to seek, explore,
To understand, to know much more.

What lies beyond the known terrain?
What wisdom hides within the rain?
What strength within us waits to rise,
When viewed through new and seeking eyes?

The question is a key, a bridge,
That spans the chasm and lifts the ridge.
It turns the night into dawn's embrace,
And lights the shadows on our face.

In every heart, a question sings,
A promise of what seeking brings.
To those who ask with an open mind,
The answers they shall surely find.

So dare to ask, to seek, to dream,
To follow where the questions lead.
For in their light, the path is clear,
And every step erases fear.

Questions not only illuminate our understanding but also play a crucial role in building resilience. For example, during a challenging period, asking, "What strengths have I developed through this experience?" can highlight personal growth and resilience. This approach is supported by the concept of post-traumatic growth, which suggests that individuals can achieve significant personal development following adversity by reframing their experiences through positive questioning.

The role of questions in emotional regulation cannot be overstated. Emotional intelligence, as defined by Daniel Goleman, includes the ability to recognize, understand, and manage our own emotions and the emotions of others. Most people are self-conscious but not self-aware. There is a marked difference between the two. Empowering questions raise your self-awareness and help you tame your emotions, making way for more emotionally intelligent insights to come through. For example, in moments of anger or frustration, asking yourself, "What am I really feeling, and why?" can uncover underlying emotions and provide insights into how to address them constructively. This practice not only harmonizes emotional fluctuations but also improves interpersonal relationships by promoting empathy and understanding.

**Actionable point:** Integrate empowering questions into daily life to bring an astonishing shift in your mental, emotional, and spiritual well-being. Here's what a day of self-introspection can look like:

1. In the morning:

Start your day with questions like

- "What am I grateful for today?"
- "What's the one good thing I can do today?"

2. During the day:

To reel your mind back into the present ask

- "What am I experiencing right now?"
- "Why am I experiencing this?"
- "Do I want to keep experiencing this?"
- "How long do I want to experience this?"
- "What's my cherished goal?"
- "What's the one step I can take towards my goal today?"

3. At night:

End your day with questions like

- "What did I learn from today's challenges?"
- "What am I proud of today?"
- "What can I improve tomorrow?"

# 8. Entropy in Action

Plans are not meant to be followed blindly, just pursued curiously. Some people get overly upset when plans abruptly change or get canceled, while others just don't enjoy making plans at all and like to leave things open-ended. You may have plans of your own, but so does the world around you. A lot of times we get into conflict with each other, and hurt each other, just because our plans for our own lives don't align. Funny how we forget why the plan is there in the first place while trying to prove a point to one another. It's there to give your goal a structure. It's there to harmonize your life and sync it with people, places, and systems around you. Our brilliant but tiny little minds cannot comprehend all the different ways in which life can unfold for us and connect us. It's not meant for that. It's meant to create by choosing, and experience by observing. If we were meant to map it all out, then overthinking would have been a coveted skill, however, it isn't.

Overthinking and predicting everything that could happen just makes us want to collapse upon ourselves and shut everything out. If the intention is to be in sync externally, then why do we strike up so much chaos internally? Ever noticed how things may seem to go south before they start rapidly getting better and life resolves itself to a new normal that is more evolved than your previous self? Our plans follow a similar pattern. You make your plans and enjoy them, but then they get disrupted and torn apart, leading to something even better if you allow the change or worsen if you resist it.

Destruction is an inevitable part of creation. The process of creation involves breaking apart the old and using it to create the new, initiating a fresh cycle of events and possibilities. Take the example of an eagle. When an eagle gets old, around 40 years of age, its body weakens, and it faces a crucial decision: go through a painful transformation or die. The eagle's talons become too weak to catch prey, its beak grows bent and dull, and its feathers become heavy with dirt and age, making it harder to fly.

So what does the eagle do? It flies to a mountaintop, far from everything, and begins an arduous process of renewal. The eagle has to break off its old beak against the rocks, wait for a new one to grow back, and then tear out its old talons. After those grow back, it plucks out its worn-out feathers, allowing fresh, strong feathers to replace them. This complete process takes months, but in the end, the eagle is reborn and can live for another 30 years.

Here's the thing: What if we, too, sometimes need to go through this kind of transformation? I am not asking you to go break your nose against a rock to build strength or search for pain. I am, however, asking you to not let your pain and life challenges go in vain. Learn from them so that you gain value.

You could think of it like this: If you want to become stronger, you have to let go of what is weak.

- **What old habits or ways of thinking are like that worn-out beak and heavy feathers for you?**

- **What would happen if you took time to let go of the things that no longer serve you?**
- **Where is your 'mountaintop', the place where you can step back, reflect, and heal?**

The eagle's journey teaches us about letting go to grow. Often, the things we cling to are the very things holding us back—like limiting beliefs, toxic relationships, or even self-doubt. But **change isn't easy**. Just like the eagle experiences pain and isolation, personal growth often requires discomfort.

---

*"Man cannot discover new oceans unless he has the courage to lose sight of the shore."*

*— André Gide.*

---

What would you choose? Pains that help you grow or comfort that stifles you? Like the eagle, we have the strength to rebuild, but we must be willing to shed what no longer helps us fly. How long will you postpone the discomfort that is trying to build a more resilient and fulfilled version of you?

People are more ok with feeling regretful than feeling rejected. One can find a certain degree of comfort in sadness also, but fear is never comfortable. That's why people choose to miss opportunities and be comfortably regretful rather than face uncomfortable rejection to be ultimately successful. Rejection strikes at the roots of our sense of self–our ego, and the pain is intense at first but simmers down later, while regret deepens and becomes heavier as time passes. You can replace a rejection with a success elsewhere or at another point in time. What about regret? It hangs heavy over us because it cannot be replaced. It can only be healed. This is where forgiveness comes in.

Can you forgive yourself for all the times you released things that you should have held onto, or forgive yourself for clinging to things for much longer than intended, only to cause pain for yourself and others? Forgiveness restarts the flow of love and strength, reviving a broken plan, person, or system into functioning harmoniously with all that it's connected to. You cannot live this life successfully without forgiveness because there will always be some or the other chaos that keeps the world on its toes. Nothing stays the same forever—everything changes, decays, or transforms. It's only the mind that resists this phenomenon of change and randomness. Disorder is not a mistake; it's the default. Order is artificial and temporary.

No matter how mundane, boring, and predictable your days are, you cannot escape the entropy of life. By saying "I want it that way and that way only" you limit yourself. You prevent life's entropic forces from bringing any meaningful change in your life because you are not used to going with the flow and embracing randomness. To resist change is to resist life's flow and your own nature. You really want to control something? Then let it go. True control lies in the art of letting go. Stop trying to micromanage life like a pushy manager at work or a family member at home who will never be satisfied, no matter what you do. Your only job is to make powerful choices, set goals, and execute the actions that align with them. The when, where, and how of success showing up at your doorstep is not your business.

We work on a hybrid model, where we plan the things we must be and do while still keeping ourselves open to life's surprises. Only those who feel weak and worn out by life avoid surprises like the plague because they believe they won't be able to handle it. Little do they realize they are already not able to handle their life; every day they live their fear, so why not drop the fight against change? Stop chasing your tail. It keeps you running in circles, making you dizzy, only to deplete you even further. Rearranging the atoms, people, or systems into an ordered state requires a constant expenditure of energy —which people don't have enough of. Life is an intricate tapestry woven from threads of predictability and randomness.

Randomness plays a crucial role in our psychological well-being. Engaging with unpredictable elements not only enhances creativity but also improves problem-solving skills and boosts our emotional resilience. People exposed to random, unpredictable patterns show greater creativity in problem-solving tasks compared to those exposed to predictable patterns. This is because randomness disrupts habitual thinking, encouraging the brain to form new connections and ideas. That's why incorporating randomness into our lives can lead to unexpected and creative solutions.

Every time life gets turbulent, do you bend or break? Consider the bamboo tree, which bends with the wind rather than breaking. Its flexibility allows it to withstand storms and adverse weather. When you embrace randomness and uncertainty, you develop the mental and emotional flexibility to see beyond temporary circumstances and gather the strength needed to navigate life's challenges. It's no surprise that people who regularly engage in activities with uncertain outcomes, such as adventure sports, exhibit higher levels of resilience and stress tolerance.

Randomness is found at the core genetic level as well. It drives evolution, promotes genetic diversity, and ensures the adaptability of species. Random mutations are the engine of evolution.

These spontaneous changes in DNA create genetic diversity, allowing species to adapt to changing environments. Random genetic mutations contribute to the evolutionary fitness of populations by providing the raw material for natural selection.[104,105]

Think of genetic mutations as tickets in a lottery. Most tickets may not win, but occasionally, one ticket results in a significant prize. Similarly, most mutations may have no effect or even be detrimental, but some lead to helpful traits that improve survival and reproduction. This randomness ensures the continuous adaptation and evolution of life. Populations with higher genetic diversity are more resilient to environmental stressors and pathogens.[106,107]

Randomness is a fundamental aspect of the natural world and the universe. Weather patterns are inherently random and chaotic, influenced by countless variables that interact in unpredictable ways. This randomness is crucial for maintaining the Earth's climate and supporting diverse ecosystems. Look at the butterfly effect, for example. The butterfly effect, suggests that a slight change in one part of a system can have significant impacts elsewhere. A butterfly flapping its wings in Brazil might set off a chain of events leading to a tornado in Texas. Interconnectedness and randomness are inherent in natural systems.

Don't force yourself to understand the meaning of the crisis you find yourself in, as the crisis is still going on. Often, it's only after some time has passed that people can see a more holistic meaning behind the challenges they face. You are not your emotions; you simply carry your emotions. When a crisis unfolds, carry your emotions (the pleasant and the not-so-pleasant ones) with grace, just like a loving parent carrying their kids.

At the very core, at the quantum level, particles behave in ways that are fundamentally random and unpredictable. This randomness is not a result of ignorance, but a key trait of nature influencing everything from the behavior of atoms to the formation of galaxies. Particles follow probabilistic rules rather than deterministic ones. Let's consider a rolling dice to understand this better. The behavior of particles at the quantum level is similar to the roll of a die. Each roll is unpredictable and governed by probability, not certainty.

In classical physics, we could predict the outcome of events with great accuracy if we knew all the conditions and forces involved—this is called determinism. For instance, if you throw a die and you know its initial position, velocity, the angle of the throw, and all environmental factors (like air resistance), you could theoretically predict the result every time. Can you control each and every factor in your life? No. Then why do we settle on the outcome that nothing is going to turn out well? When you roll a die, the result is unpredictable, but it will land on one of the six numbers with a certain probability (1/6 for each). All we can do is increase our odds of getting the desired outcome as much as possible. Create more positive possibilities for yourself by attaching a meaning of growth to each outcome.

In quantum mechanics, particles exist in superposition, meaning they don't have definite positions or states until observed. Take the example of a coin spinning in the air. While it's spinning, you can't say for sure whether it's heads or tails—it's kind of both at the same time, in a state of "superposition." It only becomes definitely heads or tails when you catch it and look at it. Or consider a simple box at your doorstep. Just by looking at the box, it will be hard to guess what is inside it. There are several possibilities of what it could be. However, when you pick it up, judging by its weight, you are already cutting out possibilities of what it could be. Shaking it and the consequent sound it makes will give you more information and narrow down the outcome more.

This is why we keep track of the things that matter to us, be it our finances, our time, our health. Whatever you continuously observe and track, you direct towards a definite outcome. What do you want to track more? Your neighborhood/office gossip or your own mental, physical, and emotional fitness? Amidst this sea of possibilities, observe the outcome you want repeatedly, both in your mind and as signs in your reality until it makes you act accordingly. Track these actions and align them with your vision, even when uncertainty is at an all-time high.

You are random; you are weird. But every time you set an intention and make an observation that correlates with it, you create a semblance of form, routine, and certainty within yourself and in life's events.

It mirrors the fundamental randomness of the natural world and the universe, driving evolution, creativity, and resilience. Be random at times. When you do, not only will you come across new opportunities, but you will get much better at adapting to challenges, and learning to be undisturbed by chaos. This is why some people are called "street smart". They develop the knack for thinking around the unpredictable by being exposed to randomness and being unperturbed by it. If you are not used to randomness at all, even the smallest of changes will make your head spin out of control. Scheduling your randomness and being open to it will lead to personal growth and a deeper understanding of your place in the grand scheme of things. So, allow the unpredictable, the spontaneous, and the random, for it's in these moments that we find more of ourselves.

**Actionable point:** Expand your comfort zone bit by bit by trying new things and being open to new perspectives to understand all the different possibilities available to you.

Once you have fully understood the role of these aspects of resilience in your life, you will never be the same again. Be honest with yourself as you assess all the ways you have given your power away. When you acknowledge something, you bring it to the surface and give it a chance to be released from your closet of fear. Remember, you cannot add to a full glass without spilling. Empty yourself of all the unwanted thought paradigms and coping patterns you have been relying on so that you create space for imbibing the qualities that can make mountains move as you remain unshakeable. Having read this far and putting the insights into action would have already put you on the path of becoming unshakeable, but let's look into how people become truly unshakeable.

# THE HOW

# CHAPTER 7
# Becoming Unshakeable

The word 'perception' comes from the Latin word percepio, which means "receiving, collecting, the action of taking possession, apprehension with the mind or senses". True perception is the art of receiving and allowing. Life is not about fighting against the things you don't want. It's simply allowing more of what you do want in a way that takes up most of your mental, emotional, and physical space, leaving very little room for the things you dislike to torment you. You will receive what you strongly perceive.

*How you see things is how you do things.*

Now that we have sufficiently discussed all the ways you have been making yourself vulnerable to life stresses (reminder: cut them out) let's dive into the qualities and habits that bridge the gap to becoming unshakeable.

## *Cleaning Your Internal Mansion Regularly*

When you accept someone else's undesirable or hurtful opinions and start reacting to them, you are inviting those opinions even deeper into yourself. It's like getting a wound on the surface of your skin—it's easy to brush off at first, right? But the more you scratch it, the deeper it goes, making it harder and longer to heal. So, don't scratch your wounds. Don't put salt on them by reacting even more. Remember that what people tell you is influenced by their own personal experiences and viewpoints. Not yours. You can still be respectful without internalizing their perspective.

What often happens is that people feel the need to prove a point, especially when their ego is hurt or when their core wounds, like guilt or shame, get triggered. These emotional reactions lead to arguments, where the goal becomes proving yourself right. But ask yourself—do you want to be right, or do you want to be happy? You can choose. You don't always have to prove a point. Sometimes, it's better to let it go. Yes, there will be times when something must be said, but if you give yourself time to respond thoughtfully, you'll find the right words and approach. Answer the question someone is posing to you internally first. Once you've processed it, you can address it appropriately without needing to defend or soothe your ego. Constantly trying to do so only agitates you further. Now, imagine the strings of a guitar. If you tune the strings too tightly, the note becomes too sharp, and the string is at risk of breaking. However, if the string is too loose, there's no structure, and you can't play music properly. The same applies to life—you need balance. You need a certain level of groundedness while staying flexible enough to create favorable circumstances effortlessly, plucking the strings and guiding them as needed.

Opposing opinions or skepticism from others often hit us hardest when some part of us has already considered or feared the same thing. If we have a strong emotional reaction, it's likely because, at some level, we believe or fear that opinion to be true. These unresolved thoughts or doubts exist subconsciously, even if consciously, we've decided differently. When someone else brings them up, it stirs us because of these internal conflicts. However, once you've resolved those doubts within yourself, external opinions won't affect you as much. When the issue is settled internally, external comments lose their power to upset you. The charge comes from unresolved wounds, but when you heal them, they no longer control your reactions. Remember, there's no one to change but yourself. Don't carry yesterday's burdens into today—it's like scratching the wound deeper, and you don't want to do that.

**Actionable point:** Start and end your day on a high note. Commit to a mental, emotional, and physical health routine for at least 60 minutes (30 minutes in the morning and 30 minutes at night). Before going to bed you can stretch, plank, exercise or give yourself a foot massage as part of the physical routine. For the mental component, you can plan the 1-3 things you will do tomorrow and visualize how well it will play out. For the emotional component, tell yourself the things you felt you really needed to hear today. Wake up in the morning, state the 3 things you are grateful for, 3 reasons why you deserve the best, and the 3 things you are going to do today. Follow this up with meditation for 10 minutes and some physical exercise like yoga, walking, running, or others. This will plug the leaks in your energy supply and consequently amplify your capacity to live life more fully and freely. "Is this worth my energy?" is an important question you must ask yourself throughout the day.

## Tuning your emotions

Emotions give momentum to your thoughts. For any thought to gain momentum, it must first be felt. Feelings are tied to the senses—it's the body that feels everything. Emotions give a more palpable form to your formless, repetitive thoughts. So if you don't react to a thought, it doesn't gain volume, it doesn't take form, and it doesn't linger in your body. That's why it simply passes like a fleeting thought.

By creating a gap between the thought and the space it takes up inside you, you're stopping those resistant, disempowering thoughts from gaining body. Don't give them more power by dwelling on them. And if you do feel them, release them.

- ❖ Release them from your body using your breath.
- ❖ Release them with movement.
- ❖ Release them with a smile.
- ❖ Release them with a glass of water.
- ❖ Release them by stepping into nature.
- ❖ Release them by giving yourself a high-five for getting this far.
- ❖ Release them by thanking the people who have shown you love and support.
- ❖ Release them, knowing how miraculous the mind truly is.

Release them by reminding yourself you're here for the experience, and the outcome you want is just another experience. The fear? It's just an experience too. It doesn't own you, and it has no claim over you—unless you choose to identify with it.

### *Nourish yourself with gratitude*

Everyone hears about the importance of gratitude. Yes, be grateful for the good things in your life. But what about the bad things—the hard lessons, the pain, the hurtful memories? Why should you be grateful for those too?

It's crucial to be thankful for these experiences because they also have something to teach you. Every challenge contains a lesson that can help you grow, understand yourself better, and avoid repeating the same mistakes. You won't be able to learn from these experiences until you dissect them, understand them, and acknowledge the role they played in your development. When you add a meaning to something that shows there was something to gain, you lower your resistance and disdain towards that experience and life. Find the silver lining of having had that experience. It does not stop here, though. The next part is crucial. When you truly forgive yourself and others, you can see the event for what it was—a lesson. Feel grateful for that lesson, even if it was harsh. It taught you, and through it, you have become stronger. Forgive yourself, forgive the other person, and appreciate the knowledge gained from that experience.

It's also important to understand that no one walks away from a painful experience completely unscathed. Even if someone appears unaffected on the outside, they may still carry emotional or mental trauma. But it's not for you to compare your wounds with theirs. Instead, focus on being grateful for the lesson and the strength it has given you. Once you've learned and grown from that experience, no one can hurt you in the same way again. It has become a step in your personal evolution, and if you can be truly grateful for it, you've become a bigger, stronger version of yourself.

You're not here to protect your ego or build an image that can be washed away overnight. What truly matters is the mental and emotional resilience you develop through life's lessons. No one can take that away from you, and it's far more valuable than any external image.

**Actionable point:** Count your blessings every day, even on the shitty days there will always be something or the other to be thankful for. When you are grateful for even the smallest of things, you will realize how supported and abundant you really are even before your current desires are fulfilled.

### *Cultivating safety*

The number one thing people really need to cultivate is the feeling of safety. We often chase after love, money, prosperity, and other external things for safety, but none of those things will come to us if we don't already feel safe. In the absence of safety, our core limbic system—the reptilian brain, the gatekeeper—will not allow other experiences to enter our systems. Once safety is established in any situation, our bodies and nervous systems become regulated enough to take on bigger experiences. We then have the capacity to take on more exciting experiences. Our energy shifts from survival to something more productive—gaining clarity, space, and brainpower that can be used for more creative and remunerative avenues. This is the shift we need, from operating out of the limbic brain to using the neocortex, because that's the evolution we are striving for. Those who continue to operate from the limbic system, stuck in survival mode, will struggle in this world. If everything feels like a threat, your body won't be able to sustain the constant shocks. It will eventually wear out and shut down.

So, how do you cultivate this feeling of safety? It doesn't come from locking yourself in a room or staying in your comfort zone forever. True safety comes from growth. It comes from learning about yourself and understanding different perspectives. Safety comes when you challenge yourself when you strengthen yourself physically, mentally, and emotionally. It also comes from changing your environment and surrounding yourself with people who enhance that feeling of safety—people who make you feel cared for and looked after. You are responsible for bringing those people into your life. Don't wait for them to show up. Actively choose people who reciprocate the care and support you offer and bring them into your environment. That's how you build safety—by building a network. You also build safety by being creative and becoming a problem-solver. Challenges are inevitable, but you can master the art of overcoming them, growing through them, and turning messes into blessings.

Physical safety is cultivated through exercise, being conscious of what you put into your body, and maintaining regular movement and stretching. This kind of positive stress, known as "eustress," trains your body to handle more. You can also build physical safety by practicing martial arts or strength-building exercises, which increase your stamina and overall sense of security.

Next, how do you create mental safety? It starts with adopting a growth mindset. Focusing on lack creates a void, a hollowness that can be disturbing when it pretends to be full. Shifting from a lack mindset to a growth mindset is essential for mental safety. Mental safety also comes from holding your ground and not being swayed by other people's drama, gossip, or negativity. It's about your "mental diet"—the inputs you allow into your mind. What kind of media do you consume? What kind of TV shows, movies, or content do you watch? These choices shape your perceptions, which, in turn, shape your sense of safety. If you perceive the world as a battleground, you won't feel safe. If you see it as a playground, you'll feel happy and excited to be here.

Emotional safety, on the other hand, revolves around love—how you show up for yourself and how much effort you put into nurturing the relationships that matter. It's important to remember that relationships are always a two-way street. You can't expect to give without receiving anything in return. Take an audit of your relationships. Which ones are one-sided? Which ones are nurturing and have the potential to grow? Focus on the relationships that nurture you, and be grateful for them. This amplifies the feeling of love and being cared for, which amplifies your sense of safety.

Last, spiritual safety is about understanding that there is no real power to hurt you. Fear comes from believing in the power to hurt, but everything in the universe is ultimately one. We weren't created to be punished, but to purify ourselves, learn, and experience the thrill of being alive. Spiritually, safety comes from cleansing yourself—physically, mentally, and emotionally. Keep your environment and hygiene clean. Speak your truth, express yourself authentically, and connect with nature. Observe that there are masculine as well as feminine traits expressed in each one of us to varying degrees and honor them.[108,109] Let your prayer to God or the universe be about gratitude instead of just a shopping list. Let all that you do be done in love as that is what God really is —omnipresent, loving, and fulfilled existence.

Raise your energy. The more you operate from a place of fear, jealousy, and anger, the more you're shooting yourself in the foot. Believe that the best things are already happening. You are the operant power in your reality. You are the one choosing to breathe, live, and create your life. You are the main character in your life, but that doesn't mean you become narcissistic. Everyone is the main character of their own lives. We are here to collaborate, not compete. We are here to make amazing memories. Remember, there is no real power to hurt. The only way something can hurt you is if you allow it by creating a hole in yourself through fear. Plug that hole with strength, courage, love, and faith. When you do, nothing can truly hurt or destroy you. Even if you get bruised, nothing can take away what you hold inside.

## *Releasing judgment*

We readily rush into watching movies, shows, and videos on the screens to feel good, fresh, and entertained but refrain from watching our own possible life stories or dreams in our minds because we attach a sense of judgment and pressure to act out those dreams in reality. The fear of not achieving a dream sometimes keeps us from dreaming itself just to avoid any hurt, and instead, the fear plays out as nightmares.

Judgment is the barricade between where you are and where you want to be. People think you need judgment to make good choices. You don't. Judgment separates, pressurizes, and condemns based on rules and norms, whereas discernment supports and selects based on one's experience and wisdom. A simple example of this is: I need to do this (Judgement) vs. I want to do this (Discernment). When choosing for yourself, use the shoulder of discernment and not the shackles of judgment. If you are weighed down by something, you cannot give your 100% to life, and that brings you more disappointment. Then you feel bad for not being good enough, but it's just that you weren't ready enough. You can only operate from the awareness you have in that moment.

Good vs Bad. Beautiful vs Ugly. Dull vs Bright. Fun vs Boring. Right vs Wrong. Easy vs Difficult. Every day, we make judgments on the go, whether it's about others or ourselves. We also stereotype people, which is just a lazy way of putting someone in a box based on limited information because we would rather make faster decisions and not spend the time to get to know a person. The society and the brain love categorizing and comparing. We are also told that it's incorrect to judge a person, and still, we do it to others and ourselves. Judgments, labels, and stereotypes only fan the flames of polarization, driving a deeper chasm between people and within themselves, isolating them further from harmony.

Judgments are often momentary, like a knee-jerk reaction stemming from the egotistical beliefs we hold, and serve as a courtroom sentence with no room for more debate. It's a defense mechanism that comes from the human need to control, but the more you try to control everything, the more uncontrolled you become, getting in the way of your peace and happiness. If we believe ourselves to be better or worse than others, we can never be at peace with ourselves and never truly get to know who we are because we would not take the actions that could have made us great without any comparison.

It's so easy to go on a rant about people who are different from you or to bad-mouth things that we dislike or disagree with, but it takes a much more balanced mind to know that not everything is black or white. In between black and white, the entire spectrum of colors and their shades exist. Those who quickly judge others are often blind to their own flaws and come from a limited place of understanding. So, should you be giving a lot of weight to such judgments from others that stem from their standards, fears, and biases? Does judgment make your life easier or harder? If it makes life harder, then why do you still carry it? Do not make someone else's problem your problem, be their solution if you can, or just mind your own business. What you throw out into the world will always find its way back to you.

*"People hasten to judge in
order not to be judged
themselves"*

*— Albert Camus*

However, it's true that we need to distinguish
things to determine what is good and not so good,
without which standards disintegrate and that is
where discernment comes in. Discernment,
which is called Viveka in Sanskrit, is about seeing
things for what they are and responding with
insight. Insight comes from a non-judgmental,
serene place inside of us that is unburdened by
expectations, opinions, and societal pressures.
Therein lies the key to good choices. You cannot
keep using other people's worn-out filters on your
lens and expect to see a view that is unique to you.
Discern to select and prioritize without needing
to criticize. You can set limits that protect you and
your loved ones without needing to blame and
shame someone else.

You have to lose one shore to reach the other shore. Our life's desires are always unfolding for us, only to be impeded by all the "what ifs" and "buts" we use, speed-breaking their momentum. Do not be the one who chokes your dream before it has learned to fully breathe. Don't let someone else's judgment become your sentence. On the one hand, we say we want peace and unity, yet on the other, we engage in behaviors that fuel the exact opposite, picking sides and judging one another. It starts with you. It starts with letting go of the blame and shame game. It begins with becoming a powerhouse yourself—a powerhouse of positivity, creativity, innovation, and intuition. Whatever your natural gift is, you take it, amplify it, and use it to propel yourself forward.

---

*"Blessed are the hearts that can bend; they shall never be broken"*

*— Albert Camus*

---

Everyone has a creative genius. The only reason people don't recognize theirs is because they've been harshly judged based on a narrow definition of intelligence, creativity, and success. So they end up believing that whatever they have is not enough. That's the darkness you must emerge from. The first step to curbing judgment toward others is to stop judging yourself. If you're doing it to others, you're likely doing it to yourself. No one is above or beneath you. Righteousness won't protect you. What makes you invincible is the dignity, acceptance, and self-respect you allow yourself to have. That is the true fabric of your strength.

**Actionable point:** Get out of these thought loops that keep you stuck, fearful, and annoyed. Here are empowering questions and cognitive reframes to help break each of the thought loops:

1. Fear of Rejection Loop

   "What if they reject me?" → "I'm not good enough to be accepted." → "It's safer not to put myself out there."

   **Empowering Question**: *"How can I fully*

*accept and treat myself right now,
regardless of others' opinions?"*

**Reframe**: *"I am there for myself, I accept
myself, and I know I will be accepted by the
right people, at the right place, at the right
time."*

2.  Negative Body Image Loop

    "My body isn't good enough." → "I'll never
    look the way I want." → "It's just going to get
    worse."

    **Empowering Question**: *"What's the one
    really good thing about my body and why is
    it special?"*

    **Reframe**: *"I love and appreciate my body
    for all that it does for me regardless of
    imperfections."*

3.  Unforgiveness Loop

    "They hurt me." → "I can't forgive them." →
    "I'll never let go of this pain."

    **Empowering Question**: *"Is my past pain
    more important than my current and future
    happiness?"*

**Reframe**: *"I release the past and free myself from it. I choose to forgive myself and everyone else who caused me pain."*

## *Choosing with trust*

It all boils down to two things. The only free will we have is the ability to make a choice in the moment and change one moment from the next. That's the only real freedom we possess—the freedom to change ourselves, and in doing so, change our circumstances. The second key is trust. With every choice, there's a need to trust in something. You either trust in the good or the bad. Even the most hopeless people have faith that things are hopeless and that nothing will ever change. So, trust is always present, but it depends on what you're placing your trust in.

It's a choice: do you trust that things are always working out for you, or that the world is cruel and nothing will change? Some people choose the latter because they feel that believing in something good will set them up for disappointment. In essence, they're choosing to avoid disappointment in the future by feeling disappointed every day. Every morning, they wake up and the same reality confirms that belief, making every day harder. Yes, when you trust good things are happening for you, it can be challenging when something terrible occurs. But you're spending so many more days in joy and happiness that, once you master your nervous system, those few tough days won't knock you down. You'll have saved enough energy and strength within yourself to get through them. On the other hand, if you live in hopelessness or depression every day, there's little scope for you to handle any worst-case scenarios because you were already depleted to begin with. It's all in the choice—it doesn't matter who you are, where you are, or how old you are. It's the choice to trust in the good or to trust in the bad for yourself.

Always trust in the good. Always trust that things are working out for you. If you truly want things to work out, trust that they will. Life, of course, will insert its twists and turns to make your story interesting. It's rarely a linear path. Life doesn't unfold in a straight line because we are not one-dimensional beings. We're connected to everything—each other, the earth, animals, the sun, the stars, and the planets. These connections are part of something much bigger than we can comprehend. Trying to control everything and then feeling bad when things don't go as planned is a recipe for disappointment. You need to ask yourself what matters more: is it the ultimate goal, or is it the exact step-by-step process of achieving that goal? Once you gain clarity on what you truly want, you can adjust your expectations. Why does it matter if everything doesn't happen exactly as you envisioned? Why not leave some space for randomness, for the universe to deliver something even better than what you had planned?

There are times when you need to be fixed and certain, but there are also times when you need to let go and move with the flow. The question is: who or what do you trust? Ultimately, trust is about well-being —the well-being of yourself and others. When you trust in your own well-being, you are also trusting in your capacity to help others. A happy, healthy person has a much greater ability to positively impact those around them. Even if you don't actively go out to help people, just being happy can inspire someone else to improve their life. Your presence alone can motivate someone to smile or make a small change in their own life, perhaps something they haven't done in a while.

That's the power of someone who is genuinely working on themselves. And that's why it's more important than ever to take this seriously and start doing the inner work today.

## *Acceptance and dopamine*

People often start and stop things without completing them because they're just chasing that dopamine high. When they see something shiny, inspiring, or motivational, they get all pumped up. It's that rush of excitement that comes. But when they reach the phase of stretching themselves to get to their goal, the dopamine wears off. At that point, they feel bogged down and begin to doubt themselves. They might feel like they're not enough to reach the top, so they go back to the start. They pick something new, get high on it, and then find themselves back in that stretch, before moving on to the next thing. This need for short-term gratification is why we leave so much of our lives and dreams incomplete—because we aren't used to the feeling of carrying on without seeing results or materializing our dreams.

If you can cultivate that feeling of fulfillment inside, you'll have the energy and strength to keep going, even when there are no visible signs of success or when things aren't going as planned. The first step is to stop seeking those quick dopamine hits.

The second key is acceptance. I know acceptance is hard. We all try to run away from the blame and shame. But if you can't accept where you are, you'll constantly find more reasons to run. I often see people picking fights— every single day—with their reality, their circumstances, and the people in their lives. Stop picking fights. You can't win the war against your inner demons if you wake up every day choosing to fight against everything. You need to accept the situation you're in as it is. By acceptance, I don't mean resigning to your fate. I mean accepting it as a temporary moment, a temporary blip, a glitch in the long sequence of events that can change at any time, as long as you make the necessary changes.

Clarity about your current state—without judgment—activates your brain's problem-solving ability and finds routes to your desired future. When you accept your current reality, even if it's not ideal, you stop fighting against it and instead start plotting a path forward. Acceptance doesn't mean settling. It simply means you're working with reality, not against it.

In that acceptance lies great power, because it means you're seeing things for what they truly are. You know that what's happening now won't remain the same, because nothing is permanent. Everything is in flux. Even in moments of stillness, changes are happening within you.

So, accept it—no matter how much it hurts. Accept the situation, accept the mess, and regain the power to shape your life from that point onward.

When you accept yourself, you stop making impulsive decisions. When you don't accept or surrender to the void, you keep trying to leap from one thing to another, continually fearing that you'll fall somewhere in between. If you want to stop making impulsive choices and start moving in the right direction, you need to figure out where you are. Once you know where you are, your internal GPS will guide you to where you need to be. But you can't get to your destination without first knowing where you are starting from. And that only happens through self-acceptance and self-forgiveness.

Also, reduce the number of inputs. When you're bombarded with too much information, it becomes distracting. You don't have time to act on all of it, and if you're not acting on it, those inputs are useless. Only when you can apply those insights by testing them, and seeing if they bring a shift in your mind, body, feelings, and breath — do they hold value. If you're just chasing insights for a dopamine hit, jumping from one thing to another, you'll eventually crash. Even the most profound wisdom becomes meaningless if you don't put it to use. Knowledge can even be a burden as it comes with a duty: once you gain it, you must apply it. When you apply it, it becomes light, like a feather. You no longer feel like a hypocrite, and soon enough, you'll start harvesting what you've sown and applied to the ground.

## *Self-concept reset*

Self-concept is what you think, feel, and believe about yourself. It's like the lens through which you view the world—and, more importantly, yourself in that world. If you believe you're going to fail, your brain, following its natural programming, will immediately reduce the willpower and energy you have for the task at hand. This happens because your brain is wired for efficiency and survival. In its attempt to conserve energy, it directs you away from tasks it deems futile, suggesting that your efforts are better spent elsewhere—specifically, in places where success seems more likely.

It's as though your brain is running on an outdated version of software, programmed to avoid pain and discomfort at all costs. And where does your brain believe you're safest? For your brain, your comfort zone is the safest zone. This zone is familiar, predictable, and, most importantly, low risk. However, this primal instinct keeps you stuck in mediocrity. If you're not stretching yourself beyond what you know, you're not evolving. And in the grand design of life, if you're not growing, you're not truly living.

Let me give you an analogy to help you understand this better. Your self-concept is like a thermostat in a house. If you've set the thermostat to 68°F, no matter how warm it gets outside, the thermostat will work to bring the temperature back down to 68°F. In the same way, your self-concept regulates your actions, decisions, and ambitions. If you believe you're only capable of achieving the "average," your brain will make sure your efforts match that internal setting, pulling you back whenever you try to exceed that expectation. But what if you could reprogram that thermostat to aim higher? This is where self-awareness and intentional change come in.

Self-concept is heavily influenced by self-talk. Imagine your brain as a powerful computer, and your words as the code that programs it. If you constantly tell yourself, "I can't do this" or "I'm not good enough," you're essentially feeding your brain negative commands, and it will execute accordingly. On the other hand, positive self-talk can change how your brain perceives challenges. Neuroscience shows that when you repeatedly affirm something about yourself, you start forming new neural pathways. This happens through a process called neuroplasticity, and it's how the brain rewires itself. With enough repetition, your new beliefs about yourself become your default settings, just like updating software on your phone. For example, imagine two students preparing for an important exam. One repeatedly tells herself, "I'm not good at this subject. I'm probably going to fail." The other says, "This subject is challenging, but I'm capable of learning and improving." The first student's brain, hearing the self-defeating message, starts saving energy and motivation for another task, reinforcing avoidance behaviors. The second student, on the other hand, primes her brain to seek out solutions and resources. Over time, the first student avoids studying, and the second continues to make progress, even if small at first. The fine difference is their self-concept and self-talk.

There is no end to the sadness one can experience and there is no limit to the happiness one can experience either. Which side of this spectrum do you want to be on? That rests solely on the perspective you set in your mind and the language you use to express that perspective.

**Actionable point:** What is the first thing you are telling yourself when you wake up? List out the qualities of the person you want to be. Tell yourself all the things you are have been wanting to hear from others so that you stop seeking external validation. Throughout the day catch the negative words you are using for yourself or your life, acknowledge that it's an old pattern that does not serve you, and pick a new word that you want to strongly associate with. Every time you find yourself going off track simply chant the word and your brain will reroute you in the right direction. For example, if you're an angry or anxious person, a simple word for you might be calm or neutral. One word will do. Repeat it. Be it.

### *Put your goals behind you*

When you write your goals as if they've already been achieved, you are essentially reshaping your identity and your belief system. You begin to act from a place of success, confidence, and certainty rather than from a place of lack, fear, or anxiety.

Research by Locke and Latham on goal-setting theory shows that framing goals as achievable and as a part of one's identity significantly increases motivation, focus, and long-term commitment.[110]

For many of us, pursuing our goals feels like pushing a boulder uphill. Every step forward is hard work, a constant struggle to push that boulder higher. But when you frame your goals in the past tense, it's as if the boulder is no longer something you must carry. The practice of seeing your goals as already achieved turns your mindset from one of striving into one of trust. You are no longer battling against the weight of what you must do; instead, you are guided by the belief that you have already done it. This aligns your brain's neural pathways to act accordingly, making success feel like a natural outcome rather than a distant, overwhelming challenge.

Neuroscientific research on mental rehearsal, often used by top athletes, shows similar results. When athletes visualize their performance as if it has already happened—focusing on the feeling of victory or achieving their personal best—they activate the same neural networks as they would during the actual event. This primes their brains to execute at that level when the time comes. The same concept applies here: by repeatedly affirming your goals as already behind you, your brain primes itself to act in alignment with that outcome.

This practice of writing your goals in the past tense does more than just offer a mental shortcut; it builds long-term resilience and emotional stability. Individuals who engage in regular self-affirmation techniques, such as writing or visualizing their success, experience lower levels of stress, increased psychological well-being, and a greater sense of control over their lives.[111] Over time, these effects accumulate, leading to a deep-seated belief in your ability to handle challenges with ease and confidence.

By shifting the narrative from "I need to achieve this" to "I have already achieved this," you begin to internalize a sense of certainty. You no longer face your goals with fear or apprehension; instead, you approach them from a position of strength, knowing that they are an inevitable part of who you are.

Consider your goals as if they are a river. When we see our goals as something far off—upstream, difficult to reach—we exhaust ourselves swimming against the current. We fight the flow, constantly feeling as though we're not getting anywhere. But when we see our goals as already behind us, as part of the river we've already navigated, we align ourselves with the current. Instead of struggling, we move with the natural flow of life, trusting that the river will carry us toward success effortlessly.

**Actionable point:** Write down your top 10 goals as if you have already achieved them in your journal every night before you go to sleep.

## *The Power of Time*

A big reason people struggle with self-concept transformation is time management. People often say, "I don't have enough time" as an excuse not to work on themselves. But what if you started seeing time as your ally instead of your enemy? One of the best ways to get ahead of time is to wake up before sunrise. If you wake up in a panic, rushing because you're short on time, and have a million things to do, you're starting your day like a car in fourth gear. The car doesn't function that way, and neither do you. You need to start in neutral, then gradually shift gears.

For humans, this means waking up calm in a serene environment. The best way to achieve this is to wake up at 4 a.m. before the world rises and the hustle and bustle begin. Wake up in silence, wake up with appreciation, and you'll magically feel like you have more than 24 hours in your day. However, some people are just not morning birds and that's ok. Give it a fair shot and see if it works. If it doesn't, then drop it. Just make sure that you wake up in peace and have a moment of introspection and intention before you jump into your to-do machine mode. Studies have shown that time and again individuals who practice mindfulness or start their day with intention report lower levels of stress and higher levels of productivity throughout the day. It's not just waking up like a rooster at the crack of dawn that determines your success. It's what you do with that precious time. Use this solitude to get a head start on the three most important goals in your life (one of which is self-care).

Many of us leak time—through distractions, over-commitment, or poor boundaries. Imagine you're carrying a bucket of water, but the bucket has several tiny holes. No matter how much water you put in, it keeps leaking out. These "holes" represent time spent on low-value activities—like endless social media scrolling, conversations that drag on, or tasks that could be delegated or eliminated. You need to say "no" more often to reclaim your time. This isn't about being rude; it's about respecting your time. When you respect your time, you begin to manage it more effectively. When people focus on their top three priorities for the day—what's truly important—they accomplish more and feel more satisfied. Time management is, at its core, self-management.

**Actionable point:** Don't wake up 5 minutes before work and spring into action. You are essentially familiarizing yourself with panic and stress first thing in the morning. Give yourself at least 30 minutes to warm up to your day and start it on your terms.

## *Immediate Application*

There are several versions of each of us. There's a version that gets caught in anxious thoughts, another that procrastinates endlessly, and one that is responsible and productive. All of these are different states of the same person—just like water can become vapor or ice, we can shift from being highly motivated to feeling completely distracted and bogged down. The best part is that we can choose and step into any version of ourselves that we desire. The challenge is that we often don't follow through once we've selected that state.

Imagine sitting in a car with all these versions of yourself. If you've been procrastinating for a while, that version of you has become the default driver of the car. Now, say you want to switch the driver to the productive version of you to get things done. The productive version takes the wheel, but can't start the car because the default procrastinating version is still holding on to the keys. Whenever you select a state, you must activate it by taking a corresponding action. Let the productive state takeover by turning the key in the ignition—by taking that first small action.

Follow it up with a second small step, and then a third. Convince yourself to do this much, at least. Soon, the productive version of you will gain momentum, and before you know it, you'll have reached your destination.

When you take an action corresponding to the selected state, you have permitted it to take over your body. When you don't immediately apply the state you have mentally chosen or the information you have consumed to the tasks at hand, you start feeling more burdened than before. You got wheels for your suitcase, but instead of attaching them, you put them in the suitcase and are now carrying it around, waiting for the perfect time that never seems to come along.

Each time you take action based on what you know, you solidify new habits and create a snowball effect of progress. Break the chain of pain your old neural pathways are taking you through and wire in new ones by embodying a different state. Knowledge without application is like collecting seeds and never planting them. Just like reading about how to lift weights won't make you stronger. You have to put in the reps.

Similarly, for self-concept improvement, simply knowing you need to think better about yourself isn't enough. You must put those thoughts into practice every day, even when it's uncomfortable.

If you are not getting the best ideas or are having doubts, it doesn't mean you are not good enough. It only means that you are not locked into the right state to perform that task. Instead of beating yourself up, simply select the state you want to be in and act accordingly. Remember, it's natural to gradually drift out of a particular state. No point overwhelming yourself with too many productive tasks either. You can use breaks to switch your state for a little while because that's why they exist. One version of you cannot keep driving your car forever. Keep switching wisely and seamlessly.

**Actionable point:** While planning your 3 most important tasks for today, also select the versions of you that will help carry out each of those goals. Make sure you select 3 or more different states of being in a day.

## Connecting the dots

Logic is for connecting the dots, while imagination is for creating the dots. I have to requote Steve Jobs's famous line, *"You can't connect the dots looking forward; you can only connect them looking backward."* When people insist everything must be logical, they often miss something important—they're usually stuck in their own heads. The more you get trapped in your mind, the less you observe what's happening around you. And the less you observe your surroundings, the fewer opportunities you have to pick up on things that could bring you closer to what you want. This doesn't mean you should be solely whimsical either. Know that there is a balance between logic and whimsy, and mastering this balance can accelerate your evolution at lightning speed.

*Everything is magic, and when we understand how it works, we call it logic.*

More often than not, we're building sandcastles in our heads, trying to connect dots, and getting frustrated over not being able to figure it all out at once. But when you're in the present moment, when you're truly looking around and paying attention, something shifts. The dots get connected on their own and that's creativity, as Steve Jobs said. The more you ruminate over something without giving it a break, the more you will eliminate or beat that vision to death even before it comes to fruition.

When you enter your imagination, create a vision, and then seamlessly shift back to the present moment to observe and soak in your surroundings, in the background your brain starts looking for real-life evidence and opportunities that match that vision. Your imaginary experience of your desire has now set the filter for your brain to bring up all the results that match it to the top of the page, i.e., bring it into the awareness of your conscious mind. The more you repeat the process, the more fine-tuned the filter becomes, and the brain starts producing more relevant and ingenious ideas that are aligned with your vision.

If fear takes over in this process, that becomes your new filter, and you will primarily observe those aspects of your life that feed that fear while pushing down all the potential ways you can achieve what you want to the bottom of your conscious stream of thoughts. The search results for what you want are simpler to wade through than the overwhelming list of those you do not want to experience. The latter will only put your brain into overdrive, aka overthinking. So, you must focus on what you want instead of what you don't want. The next step is to then implement these ideas with dedication and without worry.

As you do so, the logic behind all the actions taken so far starts to unfold with more clarity, and the desired result is obtained. This is because you had to take actions to create data points that the brain would then find a way to connect, explain, and deliver. This is how we are constantly reverse-engineering our lives without even realizing it. If you keep constantly swinging between the branches of motivation and melancholy, you are essentially collecting a bunch of incoherent dots/data points that are harder to connect. Thereby, creating an extremely drawn-out and zig-zagged path to your success. So, set your filters of focus with clear intention and do not waver with the transient wind, aka circumstances.

Focused and flexible minds are brilliant for this very reason. They are able to gather relevant information from multiple sources, connecting the dots to produce something very interesting that others would not have thought about. Add mental fortitude and you have got yourself a powerhouse who doesn't build sandcastles but forts of wealth, knowledge, and impact. The best part is that all these three traits can be acquired and are learnable. Perhaps that's why people who have exposed themselves to observing, learning, and exploring beyond the rigid academic curriculums have excelled beyond expectations.

> *"Logic will get you from A to B. Imagination will take you everywhere."*
>
> *— Albert Einstein*

There needs to be a balance between visualizing, imagining, and thinking in your head, and then switching back to the present, where you can simply sit, observe, and soak in your surroundings. If you can't make that switch, you end up stuck in a cycle of thinking, ruminating, and over-analyzing. You create ideas in your mind, only to dismiss them immediately, without giving them a chance to come into existence. Ideas need time to grow, and they can only do that when you stop overthinking, let go, and allow your brain to process them in the background. The world around you is full of clues and opportunities that can help you make things happen. But you need to be grounded—one way to do that is by being present, paying attention to your environment, and seeing what's being offered to you.

Engage with your imagination regularly and more positively with no attachments. It's basically creating prototypes for your logic to choose from and modify. I am sorry for offending the horror movie buffs, but watching a lot of gore and frightening content can give you a rush of adrenaline in the short term and disturbing thoughts and dreams in the long run. If you subconsciously hold fear-based patterns inside you (which we all do) these images and visuals will be brought up to scare you away from a trigger or doing something new, locking you deeper in your "safe" comfort zone. All this is done by the subconscious mind to protect you, however, unintendedly stagnating you. Immerse all of your inner senses with the things you would like to be around and experience with your outer senses.

You do not need to connect the dots all at once. Know that the information you need to gain clarity is coming to you, even if it's in the form of small clues and events that don't fully make sense yet. Take action because each outcome is simply more data collected that can be analyzed to connect more dots. The cause is the invisible idea conceived in the mind whereas the effect is the visible representation of that invisible idea. Everything we see around us was once just an invisible idea brought into physical existence through persistence. You find freedom when you realize that your life is the effect of the cause that is your spirit, not the other way around as we are taught.

**Actionable point:** Set out 10 to 30 minutes of your day to engage your imaginative senses. See it as a creative room, which you enter mentally after relaxing into a meditative state. With closed eyes, see or hear what you want to know more about or want to see in your life as if you are experiencing it. Once done, continue with your work. If an inspired idea pops up after this practice, implement it at whatever level possible (take a small or bigger action towards it). See it, do it, experience it, and you will be able to connect all the dots in your life much better.

### *Be your own*

We all want to find friends and people in our lives who love us just as we are. Sometimes we feel like the people around us are there because of what we've achieved, what we're doing, or because they want something from us. But deep down, we're always searching for those who accept us fully, with no strings attached.

The irony is that while we search for such people, we often aren't that person for ourselves. We don't love ourselves for simply being who we are. There's always some achievement we think will make us more lovable. We believe we'll celebrate ourselves only after we reach that next goal. But why aren't we the same friend to ourselves that we seek in others?

You must be your own non-negotiable friend. You must love yourself simply because you exist— because you live, feel, and are. Not because you've accomplished something or reached a milestone. You have to recognize that you're lovable first, and from that place of love, you go on to achieve things. You don't need to accomplish things to prove that you're worthy of love.

It's like energy: you need energy first to do work; you don't do work to get energy. It all starts with the energy, with the love. Don't let anything chip away at your sense of lovability. Every time you doubt yourself, hesitate, or let fears hold you back, it chips away at that belief that you're enough as you are.

The key is to live intentionally, not accidentally. Be mindful of how you treat yourself because the love you give yourself is the foundation for everything else you build in life.

**Actionable point:** Start cherishing your own existence by celebrating every small and big win.

Keep a book of wins which you update every night before going to sleep. Write at least 3 things. No matter how insignificant it seems, if it's good for you, it counts. It's not the thing you achieved, it's you. That's why celebrating the small things is more important because it reminds you how it's so easy to find happiness. The big things may or may not fuel our ego as we get attached to them. Nevertheless, celebrate. When you are used to celebrating your existence, your natural state of being is not in survival mode but in an elevated sense of calm. In this state, the body's capacity to create, do work and just exist peacefully gets enhanced.

## Detached present moment

The reason being mindful in the present moment matters so much is because, in every moment, you have a choice. You have a choice to start the chain reaction of happiness that creates a future where so many of your wishes, so many things, work out in your favor—simply because every moment, you're happy.

All you have to do is focus on the next step. But we often think about the end of this chain reaction, decades ahead, and worry about all the steps we need to take. Then we start stressing over how we'll find our way and how everything will fit together. But none of that matters right now. All that matters is the next step.

Can you take that next step? Can you take it in happiness? Can you be happy right now? Yes, right now. Focusing on the present takes away the burden of pressure, and you find yourself only doing what you're supposed to be doing, what you want to be doing. When you're happy in the present moment and are used to finding joy even in the worst situations, you're not afraid of anything. You've seen bad situations and stayed strong enough to detach from the circumstance, still finding your happiness.

When you've trained yourself to do that, you're no longer afraid of losing or missing out. You're not afraid of any future because you know you can still find happiness, and at the core of everything we do—seeking love, comfort, success—what we really want is happiness. The truth is, you don't even have to try. You just have to be. Just be present and focused. That's it. You might be in pain, and your body might ache, but you can still focus on something around you or a thought that makes you happy. It's just about having the courage and the will to do that. Yes, there will be forces, events, variables, and people who will try to pull you into their game. But that's when you remember: What game are you playing? What is your endgame? What is your strategy? The moment you allow yourself to react to something, you attach yourself to their game, to their influence. If it helps you, then fine, do it. I'm not saying you should detach from everything. No, we form connections. We stay connected because we're all moving towards a common goal. When you see something that aligns with your path, you do associate with it; you do connect. But don't feed off it. You grow with it through an equal exchange of value.

Detachment doesn't mean there's no love or compassion. People often think that being detached makes you cold-hearted, and lacking in empathy, but that's just not true. When you detach from anything unwanted or unsuitable, you're simply eliminating it from your consciousness. And when you do that, you make way for more desirable things to show up. The more unwanted things you focus on, even if you're fighting against them, you're still focusing on them. That's why what you resist persists. But if you simply detach and stop caring about those things, while still finding happiness in the present moment, you become untouchable. You become unshakeable.

That's what "nothing matters" means. You create matter. You make things matter by attaching importance to them, and by giving them meaning. Even with good things, when you give something more meaning than your present happiness, you shrink, and whatever you've given meaning to becomes Mount Everest—unattainable or requiring extreme effort to reach.

Revise the meaning you have given all the things, people, and situations in your life. Give it enough meaning to guide your life, but not so much that it stops you in your tracks. Don't let it hold you back or paralyze you with the fear of losing it. Even good things can become your enemy. It all depends on how you balance it. So yes, it pays to detach.

**Actionable point:** First, imagine yourself in a movie theater, where you're the audience.

You're just sitting there, watching the movie of your life play out. You have no stake in the outcome, no urge to offer advice to the characters. You're simply an observer—interested but not involved. Whatever thoughts or guidance naturally arise as you watch is your message, your inner wisdom speaking.

Second, think about pets. When you have a pet, you don't attach some elaborate future to it. You don't think, "Oh, this pet will become something amazing, and then I'll love it even more." No, you already love it as it is. You enjoy taking care of it because it's there, present, and bringing you joy.

Apply this same mindset to projects you're working on. Instead of thinking of a project as your livelihood, the sole thing keeping you afloat, try to treat it like your pet—something you're nurturing, enjoying, and engaging with, in the present moment. It's all about how you choose to view it, and the story you create around it.

Often, when we really want something, we end up attaching desperation, frustration, and fear to it. We weigh it down with too much importance, making it harder to manifest. Instead, why not attach balloons? Just joking, but seriously add joy, excitement, and enjoyment to it. This doesn't mean bad things or obstacles won't appear along the way; they will. But it won't matter. Approach life with a sense of ease, knowing that every experience is teaching you something valuable and that you're fine no matter what happens. There are no conditions attached. Think of your feelings as the clothes you wear on the inside. What feeling are you choosing to wear today? Are you donning happiness, sadness, or something else? Remember, feelings can be chosen. Sure, others may invoke or provoke certain emotions in you, but ultimately, it's your decision whether to hold on to them or let them go. You have the power to shift, to wear the inner cloak of the emotion you want to feel.

The power of non-reaction is transformative. It changes you and it changes your life's circumstances. Even when you feel resistance rising—those thoughts telling you, "You can't do this," or "Who am I to achieve this?"—just sit with it. Don't fight it. Label and acknowledge the resistance. It's not the entirety of who you are, it's just a volatile part of you. Simply recognize it for what it is, and remind yourself, "This too shall pass." Shift your attention away from the resistance, and just breathe. You'll notice that when you stop feeding it with your focus and reaction, the resistance begins to wither. It loses its strength because it depends on your reaction to sustain itself. Without your attention, it has no authority to linger, much like an uninvited guest who eventually leaves when ignored.

## Conquer and surrender

You can't have conquest without surrender—there's always a balance. You can't keep conquering everything in life. In some areas, you conquer, and in others, you surrender. When you surrender, you create the space to conquer again. I know this might seem confusing when compared to the idea of wars or battles, but that's the point. Sometimes you have to give up the battle to win the war.

The key is understanding what and where you are surrendering. Are you surrendering to your vices, or are you surrendering to your true self, to your higher path, to your way out, to the real essence of life—which is simply you? The real you, that is. What are you surrendering to? There are very few things truly worth surrendering to, so choose wisely.

When I say surrender, I mean dropping your baggage. Let go of your burdens for a moment— just lay them down. Even if it's only temporary, it can lighten the load. What are you scared of? That someone will steal your emotional baggage and use it against you? That's something worth considering. The more tightly you hold onto to it the more potent it becomes for being used against you. So drop it. Drop it like it's red hot. Don't burn your hands by holding onto it.

Clear the clutter. The more you clear it out, the more space you'll have for what truly matters. Only take with you what you need, and let the rest go. That's how you make room for the best experiences.

Are you willing to put in the effort to realize your unshakable nature? Things will always happen—that's the uncontrollable part. But are you going to make what you want happen? That's the part you can control.

In life, we are both the mountain and the river. The mountain symbolizes our unwavering beliefs, our strength, and the solid foundation upon which we build our lives. It represents the stable, enduring parts of our being—the principles, values, and convictions that shape the world around us. The mountain stands firm, grounded in its presence, and offers us stability and structure, much like the masculine traits of resilience, determination, and order. These are the aspects of ourselves that give us the power to weather storms and stand tall in the face of adversity.

Rivers represent the fluidity of our emotions, creativity, and adaptability. They flow with grace and persistence, carving their way through the terrain, bending and shaping the earth as they move. The river is ever-changing, dynamic, and responsive to its environment, much like the feminine traits of intuition, compassion, and creativity. These are the aspects of ourselves that allow us to navigate the ebb and flow of life with ease, to adapt, to create, and to evolve.

Just like the electron that exists as both a particle and a wave, we too exhibit a beautiful duality—simultaneously solid and fluid, structured and adaptable. We are a blend of the mountain's strength and the river's flow. The mountain provides us with a solid foundation, but it's the river that shapes and reshapes that foundation, carrying us toward our destinations, and forging new paths as it flows. The river doesn't simply erode the mountain; it collaborates with it, gently yet persistently molding it into new forms. The balance of the two, the interplay of strength and flow, is what makes us whole.

In the masculine-dominated world we have inherited—where rigidity, stability, and structure have long been celebrated—there has been a tendency to dam up the river of emotions, creativity, and fluidity. This has led to a societal imbalance, where the nurturing flow of the feminine has been suppressed in favor of control and rigidity. But now, that dam has burst. The world is waking up to the importance of mental and emotional health, of valuing people over policies, of nurturing the environment rather than exploiting it. This resurgence of the river, of the feminine, is not in opposition to the mountain, but rather a call for balance. After all, even the most formidable mountains can be shaped and transformed by the persistent flow of the river. Strength need not be rigid; it can be molded and softened by the flow of creativity and emotion.

Our perception of these traits—the mountain's strength and the river's flow—deeply influences how we see ourselves and the choices we make. When we lean too heavily into one side, be it the mountain's rigid stability or the river's unbridled flow, we lose the harmony that exists between them. We either become too unyielding, resistant to change, or too untethered, lacking the groundedness needed to move forward with purpose. To embody the state of being unshakeable is to understand that we must honor both our mountain-like traits—our strength, stability, and resolve—and our river-like traits of fluidity, creativity, and emotional depth. We are both the force that stands firm and the current that adapts and flows. When we recognize this duality within ourselves, we begin to see the world differently. We understand that just as a mountain is not diminished by the river. We are not weakened by our emotions or creativity. Instead, they are the forces that shape us, that help us grow and evolve. This understanding shapes the way we navigate life. We no longer resist the flow of emotions, nor do we cling too tightly to the security of the mountain. Instead, we learn to flow like the river while standing strong like the mountain.

In this balanced state, is when you get a taste of being unshakeable. Not because we are immune to change or challenge, but because we have learned to move with life's currents while remaining grounded in our beliefs. We have learned to let our emotions guide us without overwhelming us. We have learned to shape our world without losing our center. The mountain and the river are not in opposition; they are partners in our journey. Together, they create your personal valley, the experience and perception of which are determined by your beliefs, choices, emotions, actions, vantage points, and courage to explore.

**Actionable point:** Make a list of the important situations in your life that you want to improve. Next to each situation, write down if you have used the mountain aspect of yourself to solve it or the river aspect and the associated trait (stubbornness, rapid flow, groundedness, imagination, etc.). You will start to see where your imbalance lies. In the next column, write down which qualities of the mountain or the river you want to adopt to mold this situation better. The name of the game is to switch. Keep switching between exhibiting these traits as and when the situation arises. That is what evolution is —rising to the call of the changing times by changing yourself to fit the vision and mission.

# CHAPTER 8

# Staying Unshakeable

Unlearning patterns is a process that takes time, and that is okay. Expand your awareness of life with sincerity. This sincere expansion comes from a place of passionate curiosity and eagerness to create value. If you learn more, you can be more, irrespective of what anyone else is doing or planning to do. How you learn is also important. Just purchasing a book, course, retreat, or listening to a talk, does not equate to learning. Only when you are fully present and mindful of the lesson and apply it, is your learning complete and is of some value as an experience, as it's at that point that information has sunk deep enough and expanded wide enough to become wisdom.

One of my friends who has lived a colorful life with several experiences recounted how she flew all the way to another country to get her MBA and her economics professor on the first day of the class said "I am purely theoretical, I have no idea of the outside world, and have never run a business of my own, with that being said, let's continue the class." And we still go ahead with those teachings because of a certificate that validates your education but not your learnings. Your experiential learning must comprise the following traits and techniques:

### Silence

We are used to viewing silence as the absence of something, of sound, of communication, and of love, which is why it's so discomforting for many to be quiet and perfectly still. However, when you practice silence, you realize that it's actually the channel for a greater presence of mind and stronger communication with your real self. Silence is true presence, which introduces you to the subtle signs of your existence, bringing your attention to what truly matters to you.

When you are in love, be it with another person, your surroundings, or yourself, you don't feel the need to fill those moments up with words. Your awareness of yourself, your love, and your comfort in that silent moment heighten the presence of each of these things. When you run, you use distractions to take flight and steal your attention away from who you are and what you are experiencing. We also run from silence, being subconsciously afraid of what we may find out about ourselves and not liking it.

Silence is both pure acceptance of all that you are (the good and the bad) as well as the refusal to be tied down to one identity, event, or insult. The fertile background of silence makes every word of yours more powerful and meaningful. Silence can be used by cowards but also by the brave who know that their peace and ultimate vision are more important than momentarily proving themselves to someone.

The more loving silence you cultivate with yourself, the better the inputs you receive from your own self, and the less you rely on anything outside of you for clarity and joy. When you understand the power of your presence, you won't just be anywhere, throwing away your time, doing just anything with anyone. When your intention for yourself is clear, the more refined your expression gets, and deeper is the impression you make on people's minds, including your own.

**Actionable point:** Nurture your budding dreams with yourself. Don't go around trying to prove their worth to everyone around you. Keep them to yourself and allow them to come through. The more you try to debate, insist, and seek validation for your desire, the more confused and conflicted you will feel.

### *Stillness*

Being still is different from being stuck. When you are stuck, you can't move even though you want to. When you are still, you are making a decision not to move. Stillness is the art of bringing your energy back into your system when 10,000 things are screaming for your attention, unnecessarily draining you. When you are still, you detach from the external surroundings that are sending you into overdrive, and divert the focus, i.e., mental energy onto yourself, recharging your batteries.

What you observe expands, so when you start observing the sound and flow of your breath and the space inside you, you feel a sense of expansion, thereby relieving that intense pressure the external trigger thrusts upon you. So even though it may feel counterproductive, in moments of extreme pressure, dissolving into the nothingness inside you is the most comforting feeling of all. Meditation is a practice that strengthens this pathway of dissolving into an ever-expanding space. Imagine a home filled with the most beautiful things in large excess. It will still feel like an overwhelming dump yard if you have no space to walk or breathe, and all those beautiful things lose their value, as they are no longer enjoyable or distinguishable.

People struggle with stillness the most because they are constantly running, either running towards something they desperately desire or running away from something they desperately fear. Our fears have made us restless instead of restful beings. So even if you are feeling stuck, and the instinct is to run and wrestle away, find a place where you can be still, because it's this stillness that will recharge your battery and give you the wisdom to flow out of the stuck situation.

When nothing works and any piece of technology is going haywire, the layman and effective solution is to just restart the system. The same goes for you. When life feels too overwhelming, shut out your senses. Be in the comforting darkness of nothingness. Then open your eyes again. Ever noticed how, after closing your eyes for a while, everything seems brighter and more vibrant? Reboot your senses from time to time.

**Actionable point:** Sit still and rewind the clock by remembering every single thing you did and saw from the time you woke up till the present moment. When you get good at revisiting and reconstructing your memories, you expand your awareness and reduce the confusion in your life.

### *Lazer like attention*

Multi-tasking fragments our mind, attention, and satisfaction. You are everywhere while actually being nowhere. You have accomplished tasks, but because your attention was not focused, the task is barely memorable, insightful, and immersive. The results you get will be reflective of that, as they may be poor, disingenuous, or fine, but never truly great. You have come here for the experience of life, not to just tick off some big boxes and call it a day or a lifetime, getting comfy in your grave.

Instead of scrolling on social media or mindless screen time to escape, close your eyes, affirm that you release all judgment, and then immerse yourself in the dream you want to see fulfilled, fully feeling its joy and wonder. Your attention is your laser pointer. Whatever you point out with your attention, people will see and focus on. I am talking about your quiet attention on your inner world, not asking for attention in the external world. Whatever you quietly attend to, you embody. Whatever you embody, people view, interpret, and create an impression of. This impression dictates their behavior towards you.

**Actionable point:** When you have a task to finish but are distracted or overwhelmed, take several steps away from it while still having it in your line of sight. Say you have to finish a project on a laptop. After moving away from it, spend some time looking at all the things in the room that are in front of you (including the laptop). Then narrow your field of vision to observe fewer things around the laptop. Do this again until there are only a handful of things to observe. In the last round, only observe the laptop, then walk towards it and jump right into work. This is quite similar to the refocusing of the camera lens. First, zoom out wide, and little by little you start zooming in to improve the resolution of the image. Your perspective and vision work the same way.

## Willingness to take risks

Everyone's risk appetite is different. Look back at yours, identify it, take it, and try to push a bit more every single time. When you grow in trust, you won't fit doubt, you won't fit fear, you won't fit stress, you won't fit judgment. Who are you willing to become at the risk of being seen? What are you willing to do at the risk of being wildly successful? What are you willing to say at the risk of being heard by everybody? What are you willing to model at the risk that people will follow you? What are you willing to let go at the risk of getting something greater?

### *Unwillingness to accept failure*

It's only when you refuse to get back up again that you have truly lost. Every other moment has just been a staircase of lessons guiding you to success. Don't look at the world and get frustrated. Look at the world and get busy. It's not about good or bad, right or wrong. It's not about picking a side and digging a grave there for yourself. It's about being firm yet open to molding your mind and stance based on the flow of life and its events.

The major problem with humanity right now is that we are all chasing the means to an end, rather than the end itself. There are multiple means to an end, but in the quest to do what others are doing, we don't see all of these possibilities, and we completely forget about the end itself. You must remember what buying that dream car, spending time with a loved one, or traveling makes you feel. It's the feeling that you are truly after and nothing else. If you have no feelings for anything and nothing makes you feel anymore, you get numb and depressed. Feelings are what makes you want to drive and be in your body in the first place. Yet, we negate and berate these feelings when they show up.

**Actionable point:** Accept what has happened and renew your commitment towards your goals and your new self every morning, night, and multiple times during the day by embodying the feeling of having it.

## *Accountability*

Successful people are successful not because of luck, we cannot invalidate their victory that way. They are successful because they have successful habits, successful self-concept, successful beliefs, successful risk-taking, successful failing, and successful relentless momentum. It's not surprising why they become a force to reckon with. If thoughts give rise to feelings, which become beliefs that influence your actions and build your life around, then you are exactly where you wanted to be. Let us not look back in anger, or forward in fear, but look around in awareness.

Most media these days are vying for your attention, intending to wrap you up in their narrative by not letting you think for yourself. How much of you is really you and not just other people's opinions? Be your own storyteller who charts out the course of your life, rather than ending up lost on random shores by getting swayed by life's circumstances and people's opinions.

Own every choice you make. Only then can you truly own every joy and every ounce of love you receive. When you become accountable for everything that happens to you as a product of your choices, nothing and no one besides you will have the power to dictate how you feel. You become your own source of life when you accept everything that comes your way, knowing that it's happening so that you can be a better you.

**Actionable point:** You are the cause and life is your effect. Don't blame and judge yourself for the mess and the hurt you have experienced so far, only remind yourself of your freedom to choose a better thought, feeling, action, and environment.

### *Make connections*

Making the right connections also involves saying 'yes' to the right people and 'no' to others. But how do you make the right connections? It's worth the effort to reach out to people and initiate a connection. Even if you're rejected, it's not the end of the world as long as you get up and reach out to someone else who feels like a better match. Often, our ego makes us feel entitled to someone's attention and intensifies the pain of rejection. The frenzy of trying to figure out what went wrong takes over, leaving us scattered and frustrated. Ask yourself: Were you being authentic, considerate, curious, and respectful? Could you have done something differently? Being able to reciprocate means having the qualities you seek in others.

If you keep waiting for everything to fall into place without aligning yourself with what or who you want, you will never create the relationships you desire. No one is above anyone else. Holier than thou is just another charade the ego likes to play. No one is perfect. So it makes no sense to look at a person as an idol who can do no wrong. As a human, it's guaranteed that they did do something wrong at some point in time, but they learned from it and evolved from it. People tend to either put others on a pedestal or in a league below them. When we do this, we are disconnecting from them and missing out on a chance to actually learn from that person and their life experience.

If someone says something you don't agree with and is unwilling to listen, the idea is not to cancel them, but to simply divert conversations to more fruitful topics that are of interest to both of you. This is how you sustain bridges without burning every bridge that does not immediately take you where you want to go. Having like-minded individuals around us not only feels good but actually increases our odds of overcoming difficult challenges with more ease.[30]

Consider the fascinating case of longhorn crazy ants, as studied by researchers exploring the dynamics of group living and collective cognition. In an experiment designed to mimic a stone-riddled terrain, ants were observed carrying food through a semi-natural maze. The complexity of the maze increased with the addition of more cubes, posing significant navigational challenges for the ants. While individual ants might not have perceived the obstacles in their entirety, their collective effort demonstrated remarkable efficiency in overcoming these barriers. The ants outperformed advanced computer models in navigating the maze, especially as its complexity increased. The ants were capable of solving mazes with up to 55% cube coverage with the help of the collective mind, i.e., swarm intelligence.

Unlike the random walk model used by computers, which relies on algorithmic calculations to find a path, the ants employed a strategy deeply rooted in community and shared purpose. Leader ants, not burdened by the physical task of carrying food, scouted ahead, exploring and assessing the terrain. When faced with impasses, these leaders would guide the rest, offering alternative routes, and effectively pooling their cognitive resources for the collective goal.

What does this reinforce for us? Community and collaborative efforts enhance cognitive and problem-solving capacity. Connecting with fellow human beings with whom you can freely share your ideas not only gives you ideas about the easiest path to your destination but also makes you more confident about taking on the ride. Sometimes we do new things with people we like that we would have never done by ourselves before. The communities you are part of act as catalysts for developing a collective cognition that surpasses individual intelligence. This collective intelligence enables groups to tackle challenges more efficiently and creatively than solitary efforts. The ants, by leveraging their numbers and the specialized role of leaders, could adapt and overcome obstacles more efficiently than a computer algorithm, which lacks the ability to draw from multiple perspectives or adapt beyond its programmed instructions.

So, if an ant can learn to navigate a complex maze with determination and persistence, despite facing numerous challenges and setbacks, I am pretty sure we can as well. We just have to make the process more focused and fun. It's time we reconsider the value of community and collaboration in an age often marked by isolation and individualism. The question is not who is the smartest one in the room. The question is which is the smartest room and what can you do to be there?

**Actionable point:** Find a community that is dedicated to learning something you are interested in as well. It's not the communities we are born into, but rather the ones we choose and adapt to that help us expand our horizons of thought and experience. The challenges we face are often too intricate for solitary genius. They require the diversity of thought, multidisciplinary approaches, and the shared vision that comes from the community.

## *Understanding the Self*

When I truly understood myself, I let go of the need to be understood by others. That need had been the source of my loneliness, sadness, and disappointment. But when I gained self-understanding, everything changed—my choices, thoughts, feelings, actions, and beliefs. As a result, the way others perceived me changed too. A large part of communication is non-verbal. So, I didn't have to go out and tell people to understand me or to announce that I was happy and confident now. People picked up on it. They could see it, feel it, and naturally wanted to associate with that energy. Opportunities began to flow effortlessly toward me. The people I wanted to be around appeared in my life naturally because I was embodying the kind of person I wanted to be. You don't want to be bogged down by someone who is putting in very little effort towards you or someone who is broken because if you're attracted to that; it means you're broken too.

When you truly know yourself, you understand that the self is all there is. Everything else is a manipulation or a game played by the self. Reality is the world created for you, by you, and through you. You might just be living your life but still end up as a pawn in someone else's chess game, only because we are all interconnected in mysterious ways. The more you focus on other people's actions, words, and choices, the less you focus on yourself. And whatever you focus on expands in your life. Why do people say, "Focus on your goal"? Because whatever you focus on comes closer to you. You make it happen through your focus.

If you concentrate on people not loving you, on their negativity, or on the world being a terrible place, you're drawing that reality closer and closer to yourself. Why? Because you are telling your brain what to find. Whatever you throw your mental flashlight of attention on, you illuminate, i.e., bring to life and make visible. But the more you focus on knowing who you are, on understanding your strengths, on applying those strengths, and on becoming the person you want to be, that's who you will become. You'll start developing the same habits, thoughts, feelings, and opportunities as the person you aspire to be. It's not time that molds you into a better person—it's your focus. Time and space are merely showing you what needs to change or what you need to learn. That learning is **self-realization**.

It's asking you to wake up from the daydream or nightmare you're in and take meaningful steps with full conviction in yourself. And that conviction comes from the beliefs you cultivate within. You can create any belief (which is congruent with the natural laws of physics and biology)—this is one of the bizarre aspects of reality. You don't have to be defined by your past unless you choose to be. A lot of people suffer because they cling to the pain of their past and keep bringing it into the present. But you don't have to do that. Every single moment is a fresh canvas. Even if you did something wrong or weren't satisfied with your choices, it's okay—

start again. Think more clearly, consider what you can do better, and just do it.

It's the judgment of your past actions that makes you feel guilty for the rest of your life. Don't sentence yourself to life imprisonment in the mental torture of "should have," "could have," or "would have." It's just a mental prison, and the only way to break out is to show yourself—the jury—that you are not that person anymore. You're not someone who wishes ill upon themselves or self-sabotages. You are someone who cares deeply about your well-being and the well-being of those around you. When you start showing up as that person, even during tough times, when you cultivate that change within, opportunities for "prison breaks" will appear. The ball is in your court. Will you play with it? Will you have fun with it? Will you take control of the game, or will you choose to remain a victim, repeating the same unhelpful patterns in your life?

You can stay safe doing the same things, feeling sorry for yourself. But the sad truth is that this comfort comes with an expiration date. Your body will start to break down, your emotions will take a toll, and even in your so-called "comfortable" world, there will be no peace. So, what is staying stuck actually giving you?

This is why many people become chronic complainers. People who whine are often unaware or afraid to take control. It's easier to say the world is a messy, evil place than to stand up to life's challenges with courage, passion, love, and curiosity. Some people try to have these traits, but when they don't see immediate results, they give up. They start believing it's all a hoax or a scam because they are so deeply invested in negativity.

But is there any benefit to believing in negativity? Absolutely not. Is there a benefit to thinking critically? Yes, of course. There is a difference between negative thinking and critical thinking. Critical thinking is objective, while negative thinking is emotional. The intention behind critical thinking is to solve and build things while that of negative thinking is to dissolve and destroy. Importantly, critical thinkers are open-minded and welcome multiple perspectives, adjusting their conclusions based on new information. Negative thinking is closed-minded as it tends to shut down possibilities, focusing only on why things won't work, thereby, feeding the fear inside them.

Fear is what controls and manipulates people, and many use fear to gain power. Every time you're afraid, you give away your power to whoever or whatever is using that fear against you. It could be your own ego, your mind, or someone in your personal or professional life. Every time you fear something, you give away the power of choice. People feel burdened by choices because they fear judgment if the choice turns out to be wrong. But if you remove judgment and replace it with the right intention and sustained focus, things shift in your favor. This is where the heart comes in. The brain can construct a reality, but if you want to create a reality that benefits you and everyone around you, you have to involve your heart.

The heart is incredibly intelligent. It will probably guide you in the right direction, even if that place feels uncomfortable. But that discomfort is exactly where you need to be to launch yourself into the peaceful, desired paradise you want to create for yourself. So instead of creating garbage by thinking you are garbage, start creating goals. Transmute all the pressure and pain you've experienced into courage. That's the most significant thing you can do in life. We've all faced darkness, inner demons, and the loss of loved ones. We've experienced pain. But instead of being burdened by it, use that pain to fuel your desire to do better, to understand yourself more deeply, and to regain control of your life. Create a special, safer place for yourself and the people around you.

Yes, it will take guts, but pain gives you guts. You've heard the saying, "I've got nothing to lose," right? That comes from immense pain and loss. And that pain makes you fearless and limitless. It makes you willing to try things you would have never considered before. That's why they say, "Don't let a good life get in the way of a great life." Unfortunately, many people aren't even living a good life. Even if you play it safe, it's often not even that good—it's still filled with struggles and inner conflict.

The inner conflict comes from a deep knowing of what you're capable of. It's a tug-of-war between your ego and your spirit. The spirit knows what you're capable of. It knows that if you channel your energy properly, stay focused, and keep going, you'll get there. The spirit is not worried. But the ego, which feels unsafe and constantly needs to be in control, is always trying to conquer something. These two forces are rarely on the same page. So, it all depends on what you turn your attention to. Do you focus on the spirit, which is ready to support you, create happiness, and move toward your goals? Or do you focus on the ego, which tries to keep you stuck in the identity you've constructed?

So, what are you here for? Are you here for the image or the experience? This is a rhetorical question because if you have a great experience, your self-image will naturally be the best it can be. It won't be tainted by fear or loss. It can't be taken away from you. But if you forcefully control or exert pressure, eventually, it will crack and break. That is the choice you have to make.

Having a strong mindset does not mean you will never feel upset, a little nervous, or angry. It means even if you experience those things, you will never stay there reliving that experience. You will have the strength and the intention to move on to new and better things, which is the point of life–change and growth. Even if we are adults who have walked this earth for many years, there still hides in each one of us an inner child looking for love.

Your head may be calm and stable, but there may be some aching, longing, and heavy sensations in your body with no rational explanation for the same. It's ok if you cannot explain it. Supported by your steady mind, parent the child by gently stroking that part of your body where the sensation is being felt and repeat "I am" till the sensation subsides. No need to rush this process. The more you rush, the more the discomfort continues. No need to fill in the blanks by adding a label to "I am". You just are. You must acknowledge the entirety of your own presence before you try to assert your presence in the world. When you feel vulnerable and lost, just acknowledge and celebrate your existence with these two words.

Just the fact that you exist adds value in ways you cannot understand, so just be. Learn to be content with that. It will not make you lazy, because the 'I am' does not come from a place of entitlement. It comes from a place of wonder, love, and gratitude. When you are amused by your own existence, you are content and filled to the brim, ready to experience life, take bold actions, be able to give to others, and receive all the opportunities and love you desire, without being swept away by unexpected loss.

When you stop needing things is exactly when you start getting them, such is the paradox of life. When you trust someone or something, you draw them closer to you–you let them into your life. When you need someone or something, you distance them away from you —it starts to seem as if it's running away. That is why it's of paramount importance to feel whole, complete, and content by just your presence. It's then that the external world will start feeling more like a playground inviting you to express, share, and create rather than a battleground causing you and your desires to be martyred. Even on the days that feel like a battleground, you know there is nothing you cannot overcome as long as you have the courage to exist as who you really are.

**Actionable point:** Take a pause, close your eyes, start breathing as gently as possible, and ask yourself "Who am I?" or repeat the words "I Am"/ "I Am all that I Am" slowly and repeatedly until you reach neutrality.

# CHAPTER 9

# Evolution of You

The word experiment is derived from the Latin word 'experior', which means 'to experience' and 'to attempt'. You are the scientist of your life. Your lived experience is your grand experiment and no one else's, so craft it well and give it your best shot.

## *Shaping Who We Are and What We Achieve*

At the heart of becoming "Unshakeable" lies the practice of identity-congruent behavior—acting in ways that are consistent with the person we believe we are, or the person we wish to become. This isn't just a mindset; it's a powerful psychological phenomenon. Identity-based motivation, a concept explored in depth by Oyserman and colleagues, suggests that when our goals and behaviors are aligned with our self-concept, we are more likely to persist in the face of adversity and experience long-term success.[112]

If someone identifies as a "runner," they're much more likely to run regularly and take part in marathons. But if someone simply sets a goal to "start running," their commitment may waver. The key difference is the alignment between one's identity and one's actions. When your behaviors are identity-congruent, they reinforce and solidify who you are. This process creates a feedback loop —your actions shape your identity, and in turn, your identity motivates your actions.

*The Devoted Voters*

To truly understand the power of identity-congruent behavior, let's dive into an intriguing experiment conducted during the 2008 US presidential election. Social psychologists Christopher Bryan, Gregory Walton, and their colleagues were curious about how subtle shifts in self-perception could influence behavior.[113] They hypothesized that if you appeal to someone's identity rather than just their actions, you could inspire them to act in more profound, committed ways. The researchers set up a clever experiment.

They divided a group of potential voters into two categories, with each group receiving a slightly different version of the same survey. One group was asked, "How important is it for you to vote in the upcoming election?" The other group, however, was asked, "How important is it for you to be a voter in the upcoming election?"

Notice the subtle but crucial difference? The first question framed voting as an action—something external that someone could choose to do or not do. The second question, however, framed voting as an identity—something internal that defines who you are. This simple shift transformed the behavior of the people in the study. When the researchers tracked the actual turnout on Election Day, they found that those who were asked about being a "voter" were significantly more likely to show up at the polls than those who were asked about the act of voting. The people whose sense of identity was invoked—those who saw themselves as "voters"—felt a stronger pull to act in a way that was consistent with that identity. They didn't just think about voting as a task; they saw themselves as people who voted. And so they did.

*The Classroom of "Helpers"*

To understand the deep connection between identity and behavior in children, researchers conducted a social experiment on ages 3 to 6 years.[114]

In this experiment, the researchers aimed to see if framing a request in terms of identity rather than action would affect children's willingness to help. They went to an elementary school and divided the kids into two groups. Both groups of kids were presented with similar scenarios where they had opportunities to help an adult (such as picking up spilled items). For one group, the adult framed the request using identity language, saying, *"Who wants to be a helper?"* The other group was presented with the same request framed as an action, with the adult saying, *"Who wants to help?"*

What's the difference between the two? The second group was asked to help, focusing on a task. The first group was asked to *be* a helper, which is an identity, not just a behavior. It was a test to see whether the kids would be more likely to volunteer based on an identity shift rather than just a request for action.

The children who were asked to *"be a helper"* were significantly more likely to engage in helping behaviors than those who were simply asked to *"help."*

The identity-focused language ("helper") encouraged children to see the behavior as part of their identity rather than just a one-time action. This subtle shift made them more inclined to act in alignment with the perceived role of a "helper". It wasn't just about asking them to perform a task; it was about appealing to their sense of self. Being a "helper" became a part of their identity, and once they saw themselves as that type of person, their behavior naturally followed suit.

Even at a young age, children are sensitive to identity-related cues. When they perceive themselves as "helpers," helping becomes not just an action they perform but a part of who they are. When an action is more aligned with your identity it becomes more effortless and natural, and hence more easily repeatable forming a default pattern.

Children learn more from fictional stories that are similar to their own lives.[115] This is not limited to children, every time we see a character from a TV show or movie that has the same traits as us, that character becomes more strongly impressed upon our subconscious mind through an emotional connection. Essentially making us more likely to perpetuate that same behavior through our thoughts, feelings, language, clothing, body posture, and so on.

*The Case of the Lost Wallets*

In 2019, a group of behavioral scientists led by Alain Cohn conducted a global study to test the limits of human honesty.[116] The experiment was simple yet revealing: they purposely "lost" over 17,000 wallets in 355 cities across 40 different countries, leaving them at public places like banks, museums, and post offices. Each wallet contained a varying amount of money and the contact information of the supposed owner. The goal was to see how many people would return the wallets—and whether the amount of money inside would influence their decision.

Now, conventional wisdom would suggest that the more money in the wallet, the less likely someone would be to return it. After all, why wouldn't people be tempted to keep a wallet full of cash? Surprisingly, the results showed the opposite: the wallets with more money were returned at higher rates. Why? The researchers concluded that people's decisions weren't just about the monetary incentive, but something much deeper—their sense of identity.

People weren't just deciding whether to do the right thing; they were deciding whether they were the kind of person who *does* the right thing. The more money in the wallet, the greater the potential shame of seeing oneself as dishonest. Returning a wallet wasn't just an act of generosity—it was a reflection of personal integrity. Those who returned the wallets weren't simply doing a good deed; they were reinforcing their identity as honest, trustworthy people.

Just as the subjects of this study were confronted with the temptation to keep the wallet, we are constantly faced with challenges and distractions that threaten to pull us away from our goals. But when we anchor our identity in a vision of ourselves as someone who has already overcome those challenges, we gain the strength to resist temptation and stay on course.

This identity shift allows you to make choices that are in line with your future success, just as the individuals in the wallet experiment chose honesty because it was in line with their identity. If you keep taking contradictory actions in a confused state stemming from your conditioning, you will have a half-baked concept. And a half-baked self-concept will only give half-baked results. You are neither here nor there, not belonging anywhere. How can you belong to something else when your actions show that you don't even belong to your own deepest and purest sense of self and its expression in the form of desires? Deep-seated desires are nothing but seeds of self-expression. So don't stalk your desires —serenade them.

Becoming unshakeable isn't about resisting every temptation or challenge. It's about cultivating an identity so strong and aligned with your goals that your actions naturally flow from that sense of self. Once you see yourself as someone who has already succeeded, the temptations of distraction, doubt, or failure lose their grip. You don't have to strive or struggle—

because *you already are* the person you aspire to be.

It all comes back to the powerful question and answer that Yogananda Paramhansa's teachings put forth–Who are you?

Your personality or ego self is nothing but a whisper in the eternal symphony of the universe. It's not meant to figure it all out; it's simply meant to experience it all. When you go beyond your ego, the truth about all existence begins to unfold piece by piece.

**Actionable point:** Create a character sheet of your future self, read, and visualize this every day before you go to bed.

These are the questions you need to answer to create your desired future version:

- How would you describe the new version of you necessary to effortlessly achieve all of your dreams and goals?

- What skills and strengths does this new character need to have to effortlessly execute your dream and achieve it with ease?

- What strengths does this new character have that your current one does not?

- What weaknesses is this new character free of that your current one possesses?

- What good habits does this new character have that your current one does not?

- What bad habits is this new character free of that your current one possesses?

- What fears is this new character free of that your current one possesses?

- How does this new character present him/herself? What does he/she look like?

- What judgments is this new character free of that the current one possesses?

- What traits does this new character have? (Example: driven, powerful, smart, classy or procrastinate, lazy, scrappy, shy).

- Describe what the average day looks like for this new character when he/she is executing and taking massive action to achieve his/her goals.

- Describe the things this new character loves doing and has an appetite for that the current character hates and avoids at all costs.

- How would other people gossip and talk about this new character in a cafe?

## *Curiosity*

We all want to make smart choices and sharpen our intelligence. The biggest and best way to do that is through curiosity. Not only does it make life more interesting, but you are constantly gathering more information on what is possible and shaping your reality better. When you get curious, your brain enters into a heightened state. Initially, the brain regions that respond to negative stimuli become active. This is because the brain feels slightly disturbed when it realizes that it lacks certain knowledge. To fill this knowledge gap, brain regions responsible for learning and memory storage light up. This is the ideal moment for you to initiate your search for solutions.

Furthermore, once you start acquiring new knowledge in a state of curiosity, something even more fascinating than improved memory occurs:

your brain's reward system becomes activated. Every time you get curious, you get a fresh hit of dopamine flooding your body. Your body wants you to be curious, it wants you to learn, and it wants you to feel good, or else it would not be equipped for it. This has been happening from time immemorial, as it's curiosity and not always a necessity that leads to greener pastures.

Our early human ancestors needed to learn more about their environment, not only to stay safe but also to find better food and easier paths to travel. Those curious individuals who experimented with these new foods learned what was safe to eat and what was not, ensuring better nutrition and survival rates. Early humans, who were curious about the properties of fire, rather than avoiding it in fear, learned to control it. Cave paintings, sculptures, and early forms of music likely arose from a curious desire to express feelings and experiences, and to connect with something greater than the physical world.[117]

Over the millennia, curiosity has led people to experiment with their bodies, environment, and resources, giving them the chance to lead much richer lives than the ones who never adapted beyond the norm.

**Actionable point:** Trade in your need to control for the will to be curious. One really good way of letting go of control is to just get curious about your need to do so. Why do I always want to control everything? What is it that I try so hard to avoid at all costs? What are my results from being this way? What belief do I need to change here?

Also, read and learn something new every day. Even if you spend 5 minutes on it, it's fine. Spark your mind and amuse yourself.

### *Having a strong why*

Don't trade in your endgame for the milestone. The reason any of us do anything is to feel a certain type of way. Even if you say I am just doing this because it's my duty, you are still carrying out those duties to feel responsible, to feel dependable, to feel worthy. It's the feeling you chase, not the physical form it appears in. But we often lose sight of that, because we get too caught up in the details of how our desires unfold for us.

In the quest to achieve our goals and dreams, we often tend to forget why we started in the first place. You may already know your purposeful why, or may have a superficial understanding of why, or not have a why at all. The 'purposeful why' will fuel your inspiration and keep you going for miles even if the path is getting rocky and uncertain, the "superficial why" will give you motivation to charge ahead at first and then lose steam as uncertainties mount, the lack of a why will just keep you stuck where you are not progressing on any path. Good things happen to you effortlessly, when you are clearheaded, observant, enthusiastic, and in the flow not when you're waiting around hoping to stumble upon some blessings.

**Actionable point:** Note down the strongest "why" that would drive you to get out of bed, try again, and live again. What is that end feeling that you are looking for in all your experiences? Identify it so that you can feel that feeling now instead of postponing it and stonewalling it behind your desires.

## *Being in flux*

Everything is changing. Every moment is different, but life feels fluid because our senses make it seem that way. They conceal a lot of things. One million cells in your body die every second. That means in one day, approximately 1.2 kg of cells die. However, 3.8 million cells are also produced every second. Do you see it? No. Should you be aware of it? Yes, because it reminds us of how everything is always changing, whether you see it or not. Why does it all still feel the same? It's because you are aware of the same old things you were aware of yesterday without understanding that we choose the things we pay attention to and become aware of.

Why is living in this "present moment" so damn important? Because it's shifting what you are aware of. When that changes, the data your senses collect changes, your analysis of the experience changes, and hence, the way you feel changes. The most powerful things in life are not visible through the naked eye, but they are known by their undeniable perceivable impact on their surroundings. Whether that is a subatomic particle, electromagnetic waves, air, wisdom, or love.

Life is like a flipbook. Turn a page in your life, and realize, maybe for the first time, that you are the one holding the pen. Every breath, every thought, every action is an opportunity to consciously shape what comes next. Drawing something drastically different will disrupt the sense of flow in how things unravel, so we often stick to familiar patterns, thoughts, and emotions, clinging to the illusion of stability. Yet, the truth remains—everything is changing, whether we choose to see it or not. Our external perception creates the continuity, not the reality itself.

This is why stepping into the present moment is a transformative act. When we consciously bring our attention to what is happening now, we break free from the automatic cycle of responding to yesterday's thoughts and emotions. Every time you do this, it's like turning a page in that flipbook of your life, ready for something new. Your pen is your internal perception that works through imagination, beliefs, feelings, desires, values, and focus, which is drawing your reality.

Assume you're flipping through a blank flipbook. You make a dot on one page, maybe a few small lines here and there on others. But as you flip through, you see no image, no movement—just random, disconnected marks. That's what happens when we make a change once or even a few times and expect to see a shift in our lives. One dot doesn't create a story, and one action doesn't create transformation. It's the consistent, intentional marks we make on every page that bring the image to life. The space between the first dot and the moment we start to see a coherent picture is what we call time. If you make bold, deliberate strokes on every page, the image comes together faster. You start to see the movement, the flow, the outcome. But for most of us, this is where things get tricky.

Overthinking and anxiety only fill our pages with scribbles—unnecessary, chaotic lines that clutter the canvas. These marks don't contribute to the picture we're trying to create and they simply take up space, making it harder for us to draw the bold, clean lines that lead to clarity. We become entangled in these random strokes, filling the limited white space with thoughts that don't serve us. And for some, those with deep trauma, the ink from past drawings seeps through multiple pages. It stains not just the past but the present and future as well. In these cases, it may take more pages—more time—to create a new image, one that isn't overshadowed by the weight of the past. But here's the powerful truth: you don't have to erase those marks. You can incorporate them into the new image. By seeing them differently, by shifting your perspective, you can transform that old ink into part of the masterpiece you're creating.

To sum up this analogy in a practical manner—tune your focus. Remember that overthinking and anxiety are only adding clutter to your usable space. People who are clearheaded and do not drag around a heavy heart are the ones who have the capacity/space/energy to be fast implementors. Think with focus, then just stop, take the action, track it, improve it, and keep at it if you want to see pleasant and drastic changes in your reality. The key is to stay consistent. Small, intentional strokes every day create the change you seek. Even if the first few pages seem messy, keep drawing. Keep flipping. Eventually, the picture will emerge.

And this is the core of being unshakeable. It's not about controlling external circumstances—because the world around you will always be in flux—but about nurturing your internal environment. It's about developing the awareness that allows you to see change, accept it, and move with it rather than resist it.

**Actionable point:** Every moment is a brand-new moment. Remind yourself that whatever unpleasant thing or trigger you stumbled across 5 minutes, 1 day/week/month/year ago is in the past and there is no reason to copy and paste it onto your present moment. You are renewed with every choice you make and breathe you take and this new you is choosing better things, people, places, and responses.

### *Mastering the duality*

We live between a multitude of poles experiencing the contrast of the two. There is a north and south pole, anode-cathode, male and female, good and bad, brave and cowardice. When the influence of one pole is too strong, you get imbalanced and you must balance it out with the opposite action. Is everything going too fast? Then slow yourself down. Feeling a lot of uncertainty around you, then become more certain of yourself. You do this with the help of routines. However, if you are extremely certain about everything and don't allow experiences beyond that certainty, then you have turned your certainty into rigidity. Rigidity keeps you stuck. There is an element of flow, openness, curiosity, and anticipation that needs to counterbalance that certainty so that it does not become rigidity.

Every human is pulling the strings of his/her own life without even knowing it. Your reaction is a launch point for someone else's reaction. It's a game of intentions. When your intention, feeling, and action are anchored in feeling peaceful, in trust, strength, and belief, a person who is triggered and trying to trigger you will hit a dead end as they cannot break through you. This either causes them to drop the intention of anger and pain or if they are desperately looking to experience this, they will go find another person to trigger. Either way, you win. So the only and the most important thing you must and can do in life is to still yourself, tame that ocean of emotions inside of you, and train your mind to trek mountains instead of dragging boulders up the hill.

You can't be thinking and doing at the same time. You can, but it only breeds absent-mindedness and more stress. If you are thinking all the time, you are not being fair in your efforts toward "doing". If you are always doing things, you are not reflecting and calibrating enough. It's this seamless switch between being, thinking, and doing that births the feeling of having.

**Actionable point:** Do a time audit for each of these three categories: being, thinking, doing. Allocate specific time for each of these and stick to it. Being includes doing nothing, meditation, or simply taking mental screenshots of your surroundings or having fun. Thinking is the time you allow to plan your day and make decisions. Doing is simply implementing what you have planned without backtalk. Usually, we are trying to do all three at once, and then complain that we have no energy left.

## *Raising your energy*

Going by the definition of energy in physics, it's simply the capacity of the system to do work. In our modern-day lives that have become unnecessarily complex, the energy required to meet our desires and responsibilities far exceeds the energy generated within us. Every day, we are draining more energy than we are gaining by not investing the time to raise it to an optimal level. This feeling of constantly failing at productivity and not doing enough is because we remain unaware of how to tap into our unused reservoirs of energy and increase it. Energy exists in various forms. Let's consider potential energy and kinetic energy in the human body to understand the dynamics of this.

To grasp the magnitude of the potential energy within us, we can apply Einstein's famous equation: $E = mc^2$. This equation tells us that the energy (E) contained in any amount of mass (m) is equal to the mass times the speed of light (c) squared.

Let's calculate the potential energy stored in an 80 kg person.

$$E = mc^2$$

— Mass (m) = 80 kg
— Speed of light (c) = $3 \times 10^8 \, m/s$

Plugging in the values:

$$E = 80 \times (3 \times 10^8)^2$$
$$E = 80 \times 9 \times 10^{16}$$
$$E = 7.2 \times 10^{18} \, joules$$

So, the potential energy of an 80 kg human is 7.2 x $10^{18}$ joules. To put this into perspective:

➢ The atomic bomb dropped on Hiroshima released about 6.3 x $10^{13}$ joules of energy.
➢ The most powerful hydrogen bomb ever detonated, the Tsar Bomba, released approximately 2.1 x $10^{17}$ joules.

This means that the potential energy stored in one 80 kg human is approximately 114,000 times more powerful than the Hiroshima bomb and about 34 times more powerful than the Tsar Bomba. However, this energy remains trapped and dormant in our bodies. The kinetic energy we use to move is a minuscule fraction of the energy we contain within us. When we exercise, for example, we may be expending energy during the workout, but the act of increasing your body's vibration frees up more energy for you to use throughout the day, keeping you agile. Mental energy and emotional energy function along the same lines. Put a few positive thoughts and feelings in and that will trigger a cascade of biochemical changes via hormones, giving you more energy and enthusiasm for the day.

*Factors Influencing the Conversion of Potential to Kinetic*

1. *Mindset*: Our beliefs, self-confidence, and mental habits can either accelerate or inhibit the conversion of potential into action.

2. *Emotional Energy*: Emotions like fear and doubt slow down this conversion, while excitement, passion, and purpose act as catalysts.

3. *Collaboration*: Working with others allows us to pool kinetic energy, enabling a group to achieve more than any individual could alone, much like a marathon relay team.

4. *Time*: The more time we spend in fear, indecision, or distraction, the less kinetic energy we generate from our potential.

In a sense, our goal is to learn to manage this energy—to nurture and focus our potential energy and take consistent kinetic actions that align with our true purpose, much like our DNA evolves by harnessing the potential stored within its code to adapt, survive, and thrive.

**Actionable point:** In Buddhism, the practice of writing symbols or mantras to raise energy and fulfill wishes is grounded in a combination of spiritual philosophy and intention-setting.

You don't have to have a symbol or mantra here. All you need is a paper and a pen or pencil.

1. Start drawing a circle and keep retracing it. You do not have to be neat or perfect; you just have to let your hand go at it.

2. As you are drawing, identify the emotion you are currently feeling.

3. Write down the name of the emotion in the middle of the circle.

4. Start tracing that circle again and when you feel like you want to move on from that emotion, without stopping your hand's motion, continue to draw a slightly bigger circle on top of the current circle.

5. Keep circling this bigger circle.

6. As you draw, identify the emotion you are currently feeling, which is slightly less

aggravated than the emotion in the first circle.

7. Write down the name of this emotion in the middle of the circle.

8. Start tracing that circle again and when you feel like you want to move on from that emotion, without stopping your hand's motion, continue to draw a slightly bigger circle on top of the current circle.

9. Repeat the above steps until you reach an emotion that you are content with or is neutral.

Keep this free drawing motif next to you and carry on with your work. You can glance at the drawing to remind yourself of the upward trajectory you have laid out for your feelings. This will help you express yourself and lessen the need to self-sabotage by procrastinating.

### *Becoming point zero*

Neutrality is not about never reacting to anything. As long as you have emotions, you will react, although the intensity and frequency of the reaction mellow down over time. Neutrality is about not attaching a meaning to everything. If something unpleasant happens, instead of thinking the world is trying to punish you (negative), you can see it as just another random event, or as a part of the chain of events leading you to where you want to be (positive meaning). It's the attitude of "Yes, I would like things to go my way, but even if it doesn't, I am okay" that carries a deeper sense of acceptance, which breaks your fight with life.

Neutrality is the best reference point to experience life and all its colors because it allows it to be a blank canvas of endless possibilities. There is no preconceived bias, fear, obsession, or entitlement, there is only acceptance for all that can be done. Neutrality is the point zero from which it becomes possible to see everything ahead of you and everything behind you as clearly as possible. You reach the state of equilibrium upon becoming neutral. This is where the thread of time breaks apart and neither the past nor the future holds greater importance than who you are and what you feel right now, in this very moment. The past no longer has emotional weight or influence over current actions. The future becomes a neutral space, no longer clouded by projections, fears, or hopes. It gives you the vantage point to observe the unfolding of life without attaching meaning to events or rushing ahead with expectations.

Even in perfect stillness, the body is part of a dynamic system—heartbeat, breathing, and cellular activity continue, just as the universe continues to expand, stars are born, and planets rotate. But *stillness* is about being the calm center amid continuous movement.

If you observe a spinning top that is moving at full speed, it appears motionless. Yet stillness is dynamic. It's a seamless flow of movement, in sync with itself, and cutting through with skill effortlessly. The key to experiencing this dynamic stillness lies in being fully present and engaged, without any reservations or conflicts, giving your undivided attention to the present moment and wholeheartedly embracing whatever it is you are doing. Because at the heart of this perpetual motion lies a point of perfect stillness that represents neutrality where no matter how chaotic the outer world becomes, there is always a core that remains unshaken, unaffected by external forces. Stay centered, knowing that no matter how fast the world spins around you, you will be ok as you will find a way.

To get a top to start spinning, you need to apply torque, which is a force that can twist or rotate an object. That's why it's wound up by a thread before it's released. When the spinning top is released, no longer tethered, it finds its own rhythm, its own dance. Each one of us comes wound up in that thread of past baggage that twists and churns the life out of us, only to give us enough momentum to spin on our own accord, embodying a timeless motion.

When you start spinning no longer controlled by the circumstances or opinions of others, you drop all friction that can halt your momentum. You are perpetually fueled by your own inner certainty of your existence, witnessing life unfolding for you.

Every undesirable event is just providing you the fuel to push through toward your desirable event. When you experience sadness, the journey back to happiness fills you with such immense wonder more than you would have known if you were happy to begin with. Every emotion is just asking for expression so that it can be deeply known and understood. Every painful experience is not there to hollow you out, it's only there to expand your capacity to hold more of what you truly want because you now understand its value. Every misfortune is just preparing you to feel deep gratitude for experiencing the things you love. Just like contrast imaging serves to highlight subtle structures in your body, life's contrasting events bring into focus all the things that truly matter to you. These are often the things that you can't explain but feel so strongly and profoundly that it's hard to capture them with words.

It's such a wonderful and liberating feeling when you no longer have the urge to control everything around you to experience peaceful bliss. The delicate and thrilling dance between experiencing everything, and realizing that you never really needed anything more than your own recognition and love, is the poignancy of existence. Everything is birthed out of nothing and will return to it just to emerge as something else. This timeless dance knows no end. Nothing and everything are two sides of the same coin, existing simultaneously to create time, space, and life as we know it.

The universe exalts in the knowing of its existence and its myriad expressions. Always trying to get ahead of itself to create, destroy, and expand. Being mysterious and obvious in multiple ways. Having its own systems, processes, and paradoxes. Sounds very similar to us, doesn't it?

The journey of personal and collective evolution is about learning to tap into and release more of that immense reservoir—whether it's in terms of action, innovation, or the pursuit of our highest goals. Our evolution does not lie in wondering when the economy will tank, rather, it stems from our ability to unlock greater levels of energy within ourselves and channel it towards activities and innovations that take us to the next frontier. But that is a discussion for another time, perhaps another book.

Until then, soak in all that you have absorbed from this book and get great at applying it so that you get introduced to the version of yourself you have been hoping to meet all this while. The one who is everything you have ever wanted to be—

the mountain and the river, the valiant and vulnerable, the you and the I am.

# STAYING CONNECTED

The problem with most self-help books is that they offer a wonderful reading experience but they do not come with a system to keep the readers accountable for implementing the insights given. This is why self-development often turns into shelf-development. You know all the things you should do but haven't gotten around to doing them.

We are social creatures, constantly being driven by one another. Monkey see, monkey do. When you are in a community of like-minded individuals you will align your monkey mind toward your goals with focused clarity. Anytime you slip there will be others you can seek inspiration and strength from to get back up again. Whereas old toxic social circles will lock you back into the old coping patterns preventing change. There are some communities we are born into and there are some that we opt into. If you would like to opt into mine to stay accountable, learn something new, celebrate, and seek further guidance, you can visit the following page:

If you don't want to opt in just yet but want to remain connected by consuming more of my writing before the next book releases, you can sign up for my newsletter here:

I hope you had as much fun reading and resonating with this book as I had creating it. I am happy and blessed to have the chance to connect with each one of you through this experience.

Until next time,

Nidhi

# ABOUT THE AUTHOR

Hi, I am Nidhi Kona. I have played a lot of roles in my life. I have been a molecular biologist who has had the privilege of working on cutting-edge gene editing research in the UK. I have also been a scientific writer who has written several research papers for notable scientists and pharma companies. These along with my cherished roles as a daughter, friend, and explorer have brought me immense joy by challenging me to recognize my strengths and harness them in an increasingly overwhelming world.

We live in a society where one is expected to master the professional and personal front with ease and without breaking a sweat. Even though I was working in the healthcare field myself, I saw the health and well-being of my parents and friends decline. The agony of finding the right doctor, diagnosis, and solution was a painful process. Not only was I chronically stressed and exhausted managing my work and personal life, but I was deeply unsatisfied with the unhealthy mental, emotional, and physical lifestyles we take up as adults. I wanted answers other than "life is hard" and that is when I dove deep into exploring the human potential, what actually makes us sick, and the ways to repair and strengthen our psyche and the body by tapping into the innate power within.

I have and will always consider myself to be an eternal learner hungry for knowledge that can bring a profound change in how we live our precious lives. I thank all my mentors and guides for not only imparting me wisdom but also for inspiring and opening my eyes to all the wonderful possibilities that exist for us, should we choose to pursue them. It is an honor that by applying the techniques shared in this book I have been able to guide and pull a lot of individuals out of their dark times. However, it is time that a lot more people receive this gift of being courageous enough to live a happy and healthy life authentically in a world of filters and counterfeits. This book is a medium of effecting that change by connecting to as many people as possible and helping them wake up to the magic of life.

This is my first book but it will not be my last as I continue to learn, find, and hone my knowledge. I long to express myself through my writing so that it can be of service to anyone looking for a lasting memorable change. After all, life is simply an expression of a person's spirit, and mine is an unshakeable one.

# NOTES


1. Zak, P. J. The Neuroscience of Trust. *Harvard Business Review* (2017).
2. Ivcevic, Z., Moeller, J., Menges, J. & Brackett, M. Supervisor Emotionally Intelligent Behavior and Employee Creativity. *J. Creat. Behav.* **55**, 79–91 (2021).
3. Filice, L. & Weese, W. J. Developing Emotional Intelligence. *Encyclopedia* **4**, 583–599 (2024).
4. 7 Unbelievable Facts about Ants - RESTORASI EKOSISTEM RIAU (RER) - Ecological Restoration | Protect and Restore Ecosystems. https://www.rekoforest.org/field-stories/7-unbelievable-facts-about-ants/ (2023).
5. Moreau, C. S., Bell, C. D., Vila, R., Archibald, S. B. & Pierce, N. E. Phylogeny of the Ants: Diversification in the Age of Angiosperms. *Science* **312**, 101–104 (2006).
6. Smith, N. B. and D. The Mysterious 98%: Scientists Look to Shine Light on Our Dark Genome | UC San Francisco. https://www.ucsf.edu/news/2017/02/405686/mysterious-98-scientists-look-shine-light-our-dark-genome (2017).
7. Levings, D., Shaw, K. E. & Lacher, S. E. Genomic Resources for Dissecting the Role of Non-Protein Coding Variation in Gene-Environment Interactions. *Toxicology* **441**, 152505 (2020).
8. A New Field of Neuroscience Aims to Map Connections in the Brain | Harvard Medical School. https://hms.harvard.edu/news/new-field-neuroscience-aims-map-connections-brain (2023).
9. Azevedo, F. A. C. *et al.* Equal numbers of neuronal and nonneuronal cells make the human brain an isometrically scaled-up primate brain. *J. Comp. Neurol.* **513**, 532–541 (2009).
10. Ge, R. The metatheory of resilience and resiliency. *J. Clin. Psychol.* **58**, (2002).
11. History Module: The Triune Brain/Limbic System Model—What To Keep, What To Discard. https://thebrain.mcgill.ca/flash/capsules/histoire_bleu09.html.
12. Wiest, G. Neural and Mental Hierarchies. *Front. Psychol.* **3**, 516 (2012).
13. Stein, M. B., Campbell-Sills, L. & Gelernter, J. Genetic variation in 5HTTLPR is associated with emotional resilience. *Am. J. Med. Genet. Part B Neuropsychiatr.*

*Genet. Off. Publ. Int. Soc. Psychiatr. Genet.* **150B**, 900–906 (2009).

14. Aa, T. *et al.* Mindfulness meditation training alters stress-related amygdala resting state functional connectivity: a randomized controlled trial. *Soc. Cogn. Affect. Neurosci.* **10**, (2015).

15. Wr, M. Neural mechanisms of mindfulness and meditation: Evidence from neuroimaging studies. *World J. Radiol.* **6**, (2014).

16. Lam, J. A. *et al.* Neurobiology of loneliness: a systematic review. *Neuropsychopharmacology* **46**, 1873–1887 (2021).

17. Default Mode Network | Psychology Today. https://www.psychologytoday.com/intl/basics/default-mode-network.

18. Spreng, R. N. *et al.* The default network of the human brain is associated with perceived social isolation. *Nat. Commun.* **11**, 6393 (2020).

19. Noonan, M. P., Mars, R. B., Sallet, J., Dunbar, R. I. M. & Fellows, L. K. The structural and functional brain networks that support human social networks. *Behav. Brain Res.* **355**, 12–23 (2018).

20. Do Lonely People Have Different Brains? | Psychology Today. https://www.psychologytoday.com/intl/blog/the-mindful-self-express/202012/do-lonely-people-have-different-brains.

21. Rm, A. & L, T.-M. The Contribution of Physical Exercise to Brain Resilience. *Front. Behav. Neurosci.* **14**, (2021).

22. Lancaster, M. R. & Callaghan, P. The effect of exercise on resilience, its mediators and moderators, in a general population during the UK COVID-19 pandemic in 2020: a cross-sectional online study. *BMC Public Health* **22**, 827 (2022).

23. Gabrys, R. L., Tabri, N., Anisman, H. & Matheson, K. Cognitive Control and Flexibility in the Context of Stress and Depressive Symptoms: The Cognitive Control and Flexibility Questionnaire. *Front. Psychol.* **9**, 2219 (2018).

24. Kashdan, T. B. & Rottenberg, J. Psychological flexibility as a fundamental aspect of health. *Clin. Psychol. Rev.* **30**, 865–878 (2010).

25. Willner, C. J. *et al.* The Development of Cognitive Reappraisal From Early Childhood Through Adolescence: A Systematic Review and Methodological Recommendations. *Front. Psychol.* **13**, 875964 (2022).

26. Gross, J. J. Antecedent- and response-focused emotion regulation: divergent consequences for experience, expression, and physiology. *J. Pers. Soc. Psychol.* **74**, 224–237 (1998).

27. Nummenmaa, L., Seppälä, K. & Putkinen, V. Molecular Imaging of the Human Emotion Circuit. in *Social and Affective Neuroscience of Everyday Human Interaction: From Theory to Methodology* (eds. Boggio, P. S. et al.) 3–21 (Springer International Publishing, Cham, 2023). doi:10.1007/978-3-031-08651-9_1.

28. Veening, J. G. & Barendregt, H. P. The effects of Beta-Endorphin: state change modification. *Fluids Barriers CNS* **12**, 3 (2015).

29. Sprouse-Blum, A. S., Smith, G., Sugai, D. & Parsa, F. D. Understanding Endorphins and Their Importance in Pain Management. *Hawaii Med. J.* **69**, 70–71 (2010).

30. Kikusui, T., Winslow, J. T. & Mori, Y. Social buffering: relief from stress and anxiety. *Philos. Trans. R. Soc. B Biol. Sci.* **361**, 2215–2228 (2006).

31. Lembke, A. DOPAMINE NATION: Finding Balance in the Age of Indulgence.

32. Twenge, J. M. & Campbell, W. K. Living in the Age of Entitlement.

33. The Unbearable Automaticity of Being | Request PDF. https://www.researchgate.net/publication/232480626_The_Unbearable_Automaticity_of_Being.

34. Sampedro-Piquero, P. & Begega, A. Environmental Enrichment as a Positive Behavioral Intervention Across the Lifespan. *Curr. Neuropharmacol.* **15**, 459–470 (2017).

35. Schoentgen, B., Gagliardi, G. & Défontaines, B. Environmental and Cognitive Enrichment in Childhood as Protective Factors in the Adult and Aging Brain. *Front. Psychol.* **11**, 1814 (2020).

36. Why Dogs Need Regular Walks for Their Mental Health. *Animal Hospital of North Gwinnett* https://www.animalhospitalofng.com/blog/why-dogs-need-regular-walks-for-their-mental-health.

37. How and why does the heart pump blood to itself? *HowStuffWorks* https://health.howstuffworks.com/human-body/systems/circulatory/heart-pump-blood.htm (2008).

38. Published, R. R. Heart of the Matter: 7 Things to Know About Your Ticker. *livescience.com* https://www.livescience.com/44460-heart-facts.html (2014).

39. Chu, B., Marwaha, K., Sanvictores, T., Awosika, A. O. & Ayers, D. Physiology, Stress Reaction. in *StatPearls* (StatPearls Publishing, Treasure Island (FL), 2024).

40. Tendulkar, M. *et al.* Clinical potential of sensory neurites in the heart and their role in decision-making. *Front. Neurosci.* **17**, 1308232 (2024).

41. Miller, M. Emotional Rescue: The Heart-Brain Connection. *Cerebrum Dana Forum Brain Sci.* **2019**, cer-05-19 (2019).

42. Russo, M. A., Santarelli, D. M. & O'Rourke, D. The physiological effects of slow breathing in the healthy human. *Breathe* **13**, 298–309 (2017).

43. Turankar, A. V. *et al.* Effects of slow breathing exercise on cardiovascular functions, pulmonary functions & galvanic skin resistance in healthy human volunteers - a pilot study. *Indian J. Med. Res.* **137**, 916–921 (2013).

44. Shao, R., Man, I. S. C. & Lee, T. M. C. The Effect of Slow-Paced Breathing on Cardiovascular and Emotion Functions: A Meta-Analysis and Systematic Review. *Mindfulness* **15**, 1–18 (2024).

45. Corliss, J. Breathing exercises to lower your blood pressure. *Harvard Health* https://www.health.harvard.edu/heart-health/breathing-exercises-to-lower-your-blood-pressure (2023).

46. Magnon, V., Dutheil, F. & Vallet, G. T. Benefits from one session of deep and slow breathing on vagal tone and anxiety in young and older adults. *Sci. Rep.* **11**, 19267 (2021).

47. The Magnetic Field Produced by the Heart and Its Influence on MRI - Xu - 2017 - Mathematical Problems in Engineering - Wiley Online Library. https://onlinelibrary.wiley.com/doi/10.1155/2017/3035479.

48. Roth, B. J. Biomagnetism: The First Sixty Years. *Sensors* **23**, 4218 (2023).

49. Brain mechanisms underlying the modulation of heart rate variability when accepting and reappraising emotions - PubMed. https://pubmed.ncbi.nlm.nih.gov/39138266/.

50. Arakaki, X. *et al.* The connection between heart rate variability (HRV), neurological health, and cognition: A literature review. *Front. Neurosci.* **17**, (2023).

51. Forte, G., Morelli, M. & Casagrande, M. Heart Rate Variability and Decision-Making: Autonomic Responses in Making Decisions. *Brain Sci.* **11**, 243 (2021).

52. C, W. *et al.* Affective emotion increases heart rate variability and activates left dorsolateral prefrontal cortex in post-traumatic growth. *Sci. Rep.* **7**, (2017).

53. Wu, Y., Gu, R., Yang, Q. & Luo, Y. How Do Amusement, Anger and Fear Influence Heart Rate and Heart Rate Variability? *Front. Neurosci.* **13**, 1131 (2019).

54. Reed, C. L. *et al.* Body Matters in Emotion: Restricted Body Movement and Posture Affect Expression and Recognition of Status-Related Emotions. *Front. Psychol.* **11**, (2020).

55. Chen, Q. Neurobiological and anti-aging benefits of yoga: A comprehensive review of recent advances in non-pharmacological therapy. *Exp. Gerontol.* **196**, 112550 (2024).

56. Schmalzl, L., Powers, C. & Henje Blom, E. Neurophysiological and neurocognitive mechanisms underlying the effects of yoga-based practices: towards a comprehensive theoretical framework. *Front. Hum. Neurosci.* **9**, (2015).

57. Jerath, R., Edry, J. W., Barnes, V. A. & Jerath, V. Physiology of long pranayamic breathing: neural respiratory elements may provide a mechanism that explains how slow deep breathing shifts the autonomic nervous system. *Med. Hypotheses* **67**, 566–571 (2006).

58. Trampe, D., Quoidbach, J. & Taquet, M. Emotions in Everyday Life. *PLoS ONE* **10**, e0145450 (2015).

59. Fredrickson, B. L. Positive Emotions Broaden and Build. in *Advances in Experimental Social Psychology* vol. 47 1–53 (Elsevier, 2013).

60. Baumeister, R. F., Bratslavsky, E., Finkenauer, C. & Vohs, K. D. Bad is Stronger than Good. *Rev. Gen. Psychol.* **5**, 323–370 (2001).

61. Šimić, G. *et al.* Understanding Emotions: Origins and Roles of the Amygdala. *Biomolecules* **11**, 823 (2021).

62. Tyng, C. M., Amin, H. U., Saad, M. N. M. & Malik, A. S. The Influences of Emotion on Learning and Memory. *Front. Psychol.* **8**, (2017).

63. Zadra, J. R. & Clore, G. L. Emotion and Perception: The Role of Affective Information. *Wiley Interdiscip. Rev. Cogn. Sci.* **2**, 676–685 (2011).

64. Hecht, D. The Neural Basis of Optimism and Pessimism. *Exp. Neurobiol.* **22**, 173–199 (2013).

65. Forbes: A new billionaire every 17 hours – DW – 04/08/2021. *dw.com* https://www.dw.com/en/forbes-a-new-billionaire-every-17-hours/a-57135443.

66. Peterson-Withorn, C. Nearly 500 People Became Billionaires During The Pandemic Year. *Forbes* https://www.forbes.com/sites/chasewithorn/2021/04/06/nearly-500-people-have-become-billionaires-during-the-pandemic-year/.

67. Tognini, G. Meet The 40 New Billionaires Who Got Rich Fighting Covid-19. *Forbes* https://www.forbes.com/sites/giacomotognini/2021/04/06/meet-the-40-new-billionaires-who-got-rich-fighting-covid-19/.

68. Eyewitness Testimony and Memory Biases. *Noba* https://nobaproject.com/modules/eyewitness-testimony-and-memory-biases.

69. Zlotnik, G. & Vansintjan, A. Memory: An Extended Definition. *Front. Psychol.* **10**, (2019).

70. Memory (Encoding, Storage, Retrieval). *Noba* https://nobaproject.com/modules/memory-encoding-storage-retrieval.

71. Rasch, B. & Born, J. About Sleep's Role in Memory. *Physiol. Rev.* **93**, 681–766 (2013).

72. Vogel, S. & Schwabe, L. Learning and memory under stress: implications for the classroom. *Npj Sci. Learn.* **1**, 1–10 (2016).

73. Lacy, J. W. & Stark, C. E. L. The Neuroscience of Memory: Implications for the Courtroom. *Nat. Rev. Neurosci.* **14**, 649–658 (2013).

74. Loftus and Palmer 1974 | Car Crash Experiment. https://www.simplypsychology.org/loftus-palmer.html (2023).

75. Hebbian Theory - an overview | ScienceDirect Topics. https://www.sciencedirect.com/topics/neuroscience/hebbian-theory.

76. Keysers, C. & Gazzola, V. Hebbian learning and predictive mirror neurons for actions, sensations and emotions. *Philos. Trans. R. Soc. B Biol. Sci.* **369**, 20130175 (2014).

77. Preston, S. D. & de Waal, F. B. M. Empathy: Its ultimate and proximate bases. *Behav. Brain Sci.* **25**, 1–20; discussion 20-71 (2002).

78. J, D. & Pl, J. The functional architecture of human empathy. *Behav. Cogn. Neurosci. Rev.* **3**, (2004).

79. Gallese, V. & Goldman, A. Mirror neurons and the simulation theory of mind-reading. *Trends Cogn. Sci.* **2**, 493–501 (1998).

80. Acharya, S. & Shukla, S. Mirror neurons: Enigma of the metaphysical modular brain. *J. Nat. Sci. Biol. Med.* **3**, 118–124 (2012).

81. Iacoboni, M. Mirror Neurons, Empathy, and the Other. in *Oxford Research Encyclopedia of Psychology*.

82. Penagos-Corzo, J. C., Cosio van-Hasselt, M., Escobar, D., Vázquez-Roque, R. A. & Flores, G. Mirror neurons and empathy-related regions in psychopathy: Systematic review, meta-analysis, and a working model. *Soc. Neurosci.* **17**, 462–479 (2022).

83. Grossmann, I. & Kross, E. Exploring Solomon's paradox: self-distancing eliminates the self-other asymmetry in wise reasoning about close relationships in younger and older adults. *Psychol. Sci.* **25**, 1571–1580 (2014).

84. Why We Give Great Advice To Others But Can't Take it Ourselves. https://www.forbes.com/sites/datafreaks/2015/04/07/why-we-give-great-advice-to-others-but-cant-take-it-ourselves/.

85. Gollwitzer, P. M. & Sheeran, P. Implementation Intentions and Goal Achievement: A Meta-analysis of Effects and Processes. in *Advances in Experimental*

*Social Psychology* vol. 38 69–119 (Academic Press, 2006).

86. Schaerer, M., Tost, LP., Huang, L., Gino, F., Larrick, R.. Advice Giving: A Subtle Pathway to Power. *Pers. Soc. Psychol. Bull.* **44**, (2018).

87. Eskreis-Winkler, L., Fishbach, A., Duckworth, A.L.. Dear Abby: Should I Give Advice or Receive It? *Psychol. Sci.* **29**, (2018).

88. Alanazi, M. R., Aldhafeeri, N. A., Salem, S. S., Jabari, T. M. & Al Mengah, R. khalid. Clinical environmental stressors and coping behaviors among undergraduate nursing students in Saudi Arabia: A cross-sectional study. *Int. J. Nurs. Sci.* **10**, 97–103 (2023).

89. Ding, Y. *et al.* The Impact of Different Coping Styles on Psychological Distress during the COVID-19: The Mediating Role of Perceived Stress. *Int. J. Environ. Res. Public. Health* **18**, 10947 (2021).

90. Holahan, C. J., Moos, R. H., Holahan, C. K., Brennan, P. L. & Schutte, K. K. Stress Generation, Avoidance Coping, and Depressive Symptoms: A 10-Year Model. *J. Consult. Clin. Psychol.* **73**, 658–666 (2005).

91. Puterman, E. *et al.* The Power of Exercise: Buffering the Effect of Chronic Stress on Telomere Length. *PLOS ONE* **5**, e10837 (2010).

92. Harvanek, Z. M., Fogelman, N., Xu, K. & Sinha, R. Psychological and biological resilience modulates the effects of stress on epigenetic aging. *Transl. Psychiatry* **11**, 601 (2021).

93. Peng, Y. & Mao, C. The Impact of Person–Job Fit on Job Satisfaction: The Mediator Role of Self Efficacy. *Soc. Indic. Res.* **121**, 805–813 (2015).

94. Guarnaccia, C., Scrima, F., Civilleri, A. & Salerno, L. The Role of Occupational Self-Efficacy in Mediating the Effect of Job Insecurity on Work Engagement, Satisfaction and General Health. *Curr. Psychol.* **37**, 488–497 (2018).

95. Ozbay, F. *et al.* Social Support and Resilience to Stress. *Psychiatry Edgmont* **4**, 35–40 (2007).

96. MacDonald, E. A. *et al.* Sinoatrial Node Structure, Mechanics, Electrophysiology and the Chronotropic Response to Stretch in Rabbit and Mouse. *Front. Physiol.* **11**, (2020).

97. Kashou, A. H., Basit, H. & Chhabra, L. Physiology, Sinoatrial Node. in *StatPearls* (StatPearls Publishing, Treasure Island (FL), 2024).

98. Benzoni, P. *et al.* The funny current: Even funnier than 40 years ago. Uncanonical expression and roles of HCN/f channels all over the body. *Prog. Biophys. Mol. Biol.* **166**, 189–204 (2021).

99. 36 Questions for Increasing Closeness (Greater Good in Action).

https://ggia.berkeley.edu/practice/36_questions_for_in creasing_closeness.

100. Welker, K. M. *et al.* Effects of self-disclosure and responsiveness between couples on passionate love within couples. *Pers. Relatsh.* **21**, 692–708 (2014).

101. Tugade, M. M. & Fredrickson, B. L. Regulation of Positive Emotions: Emotion Regulation Strategies that Promote Resilience. *J. Happiness Stud.* **8**, 311–333 (2007).

102. Di Domenico, S. I. & Ryan, R. M. The Emerging Neuroscience of Intrinsic Motivation: A New Frontier in Self-Determination Research. *Front. Hum. Neurosci.* **11**, (2017).

103. Stanford University's Carol Dweck on the Growth Mindset and Education | OneDublin.org. https://onedublin.org/2012/06/19/stanford-universitys-carol-dweck-on-the-growth-mindset-and-education/.

104. Olson-Manning, C. F., Wagner, M. R. & Mitchell-Olds, T. Adaptive evolution: evaluating empirical support for theoretical predictions. *Nat. Rev. Genet.* **13**, 867–877 (2012).

105. Ellegren, H. & Sheldon, B. C. Genetic basis of fitness differences in natural populations. *Nature* **452**, 169–175 (2008).

106. Baums, I. B., Chamberland, V. F., Locatelli, N. S. & Conn, T. Maximizing Genetic Diversity in Coral Restoration Projects. in *Coral Reef Conservation and Restoration in the Omics Age* (eds. van Oppen, M. J. H. & Aranda Lastra, M.) 35–53 (Springer International Publishing, Cham, 2022). doi:10.1007/978-3-031-07055-6_3.

107. Mable, B. K. Conservation of adaptive potential and functional diversity: integrating old and new approaches. *Conserv. Genet.* **20**, 89–100 (2019).

108. Raveesh, B. N. Ardhanareeshwara concept: Brain and psychiatry. *Indian J. Psychiatry* **55**, S263 (2013).

109. Joel, D. Beyond the binary: Rethinking sex and the brain. *Neurosci. Biobehav. Rev.* **122**, 165–175 (2021).

110. Locke, E. A. & Latham, G. P. Building a practically useful theory of goal setting and task motivation. A 35-year odyssey. *Am. Psychol.* **57**, 705–717 (2002).

111. Creswell, J. D., Dutcher, J. M., Klein, W. M. P., Harris, P. R. & Levine, J. M. Self-Affirmation Improves Problem-Solving under Stress. *PLoS ONE* **8**, e62593 (2013).

112. Oyserman, D. Identity-based motivation: Implications for action-readiness, procedural-readiness, and consumer behavior. *J. Consum. Psychol.* **19**, 250–260 (2009).

113. Bryan, C. J., Walton, G. M., Rogers, T. & Dweck, C. S. Motivating voter turnout by invoking the self. *Proc. Natl. Acad. Sci. U. S. A.* **108**, 12653–12656 (2011).

114. Bryan, C. J., Master, A. & Walton, G. M. "Helping" versus "being a helper": Invoking the self to increase helping in young children. *Child Dev.* **85**, 1836–1842 (2014).

115. Dore, R. A. The effect of character similarity on children's learning from fictional stories: The roles of race and gender. *J. Exp. Child Psychol.* **214**, 105310 (2022).

116. Cohn, A., Maréchal, M. A., Tannenbaum, D. & Zünd, C. L. Civic honesty around the globe. *Science* **365**, 70–73 (2019).

117. Britannica's Curiosity Compass: The Science of Curiosity. *Britannica's Curiosity Compass* https://curiosity.britannica.com/science-of-curiosity.html.